# Planning and resourcing 'A' level French

## A handbook for teachers

by

Robin Pickering

CiLT

The views expressed in this book are those of the author and do not necessarily reflect the views of CILT.

First published 1992

ISBN 1 874016 00 3

Cover by Logos Design & Advertising
Printed in Great Britain by Blackmore Press

Published by Centre for Information on Language Teaching and Research, Regent's College, Inner Circle, Regent's Park, London NW1 4NS.

## Thanks

I should like to express my sincere thanks to past and present colleagues and students at Exeter College for the part they have played in developing the ideas contained in this book. The book is the fruit of work which has taken place over the last ten years or so, and many people have therefore (mostly unknowingly) contributed to it. Additionally, I should like to extend my thanks to colleagues at the Oxford Delegacy with whom I have been involved in syllabus development work and examining over a similar period. Their forward-looking approach has done much to bring teaching and examining closer together. Specifically, I should like to acknowledge the enormous amount of work voluntarily done by Lynne Bradley in preparing the work for publication; she had the unenviable task of translating my manuscript into word-processed form and spent countless hours revamping and moving texts at various stages during the writing.

## Acknowledgements

The University of Oxford Delegacy of Local Examinations for material from the following Resource Packs:

*'L'Etranger'* (Robin Pickering)
*'Tartuffe'* (Simon Loveday)
*'Les parcs nationaux et régionaux'* (Robin Pickering)
*'L'Impressionnisme'* (Margaret-Anne Smith) (also Exeter Tapes)
*'La violence: causes, effets, solutions'* (Lid King)
*'Les ordinateurs et la société contemporaine'* (Rosalind Forsyth)
*'La France et les affaires étrangères'* (Catherine Holborn)

The University of Oxford Delegacy of Local Examinations for material from the following examination papers:

9820/1 Communicative task (Summer 1990)
9820/3 Listening (Summer 1990)

## List of references

p 24 *Collins Robert French dictionary* (Collins) and *Micro Robert: dictionnaire du Français primordial* (Le Robert)

p 28 'Un tunnel sous la Meije' from *Ecologie*

p 34 *Grand Atlas de la France: Région Baisse Normandie et Haute Normandie* (Alpha Editions SA)

p 37 'L'Agriculture en Livradois-Forez' from *Le parc naturel régional du Livradois-Forez*

p 46 'A la conquête de l'Europe' from *La dépêche du parc naturel régional des Volcans*

p 51 'Cocktail Molotov contre restaurant arabe' from *Dernières nouvelles d'Alsace*

p 54 'Ecrins/Cévennes' from *Les parcs nationaux*

p 107 'Alfred Sisley' from *Chefs d'oeuvre impressionnistes et post-impressionnistes* (Réunion des Musées Nationaux)

p 114 'L'Exode et ses répercussions' from *Le parc naturel régional du Livradois - Forez*

p 126 'L'Impressionnisme' from *L'Impressionnisme* (Les Maîtres d'Art)

p 137/8 'Nafea Faaipoipo' from *Gauguin* (Réunion des Musées Nationaux)

p 149 'Haro sur Van Gogh et Cézanne' from *Le Figaro*

p 166 National Curriculum Modern Foreign Languages Working Group proposals

**CONTENTS**

## Introduction

# PROVIDING A FRAMEWORK

The past few years have seen a radical shift in the approach to the teaching of languages at 'A' level. The process was begun with the publication in the early 1980s of *French 16-19 - a new perspective,* in which the authors advocated a mixed-skill methodology through a specific approach to the exploitation of written and audio texts, resulting in an emphasis on the teaching of the language through topics. But it was given an even greater momentum by a number of other changes taking place both in education generally and in language teaching particularly, during the same period. The changing nature of the sixth form, the introduction of GCSE, new initiatives such as TVEI, demands for more practical courses and a rapid move towards a communicative philosophy all contributed to the spawning of new 'A' level syllabuses by the end of the decade. Further changes are just around the corner as the examination boards prepare a comprehensive review of syllabuses to meet the needs of students coming through the National Curriculum which will have to conform to a new set of general principles.

In a period of such change, it is hardly surprising that many 'A' level teachers find themselves swept along in a fast-running tide. New syllabuses demand new methodologies and new materials. Provision and experience vary enormously from school to school. There is consequently a real need to examine the implications of all the changes for teacher and student, and the ways in which theory can become reality. The purpose of this book is not to dwell on the philosophical background to the current situation, but to act as a practical guide to the teacher faced with teaching one of the new 'A' level syllabuses, at a strategic and operational level.

Before dealing with specifics, it might nonetheless be helpful to identify the major new features of 'A' level language learning to have emerged, features which are also likely to shape other syllabuses at this level over the next few years. These syllabuses may serve 'A' level or vocationally oriented courses of the kind which could be delivered in a modular fashion.

*Study of topics*

Traditional 'A' level courses all contained study of literature in the shape of 'set texts'. Now, a much broader understanding of the cultural background is possible, which may include literature but covers many other spheres related to the country of origin of the language. These range from socio-economic to geographic, artistic, historical, scientific and commercial. As part of the examination, students are required to write in the foreign language on one or more prepared topics, and generally these thematic studies are also linked to the oral test. In practice, most teachers organise their 'A' level course on a topic-by-topic basis. The effect of this is to consolidate the mixed-skill methodology and to link language study more closely to the country of origin than hitherto. This cultural dimension is further enhanced by the use of authentic materials in reading and listening exercises, ensuring that students have a broad exposure to the contemporary society. It should not, however, be assumed that the content of the 'A' level course can now only be defined in terms of topics. There are other equally valid methods of developing competencies in a mixed-skill context. A good example is the assignment-based approach favoured by BTEC, in which students have a specific task to fulfil, in the course of which they are required to undertake a range of different language activities. There could well be a development of this type of work in 'A' level syllabuses in the future, and teaching programmes will need to take account of them where appropriate.

*A mixed-skill approach*

There is little doubt that the development of different language skills is closely inter-related. Work undertaken in one mode (e.g. reading) is supported by follow-up activities in others (e.g. listening, speaking). This way, knowledge and capacities acquired in one class are used to enhance performance in the next. Not only does this help build confidence and give a sense of direction to the work, it also reflects the real way in which language skills are acquired.

*Emphasis on communicative skills*

As in GCSE, greater emphasis is now placed on the ability to communicate message - whether spoken or written - and rather less than in the past on grammatical precision for its own sake. The corollary of this is to give much greater priority to use of the foreign language in the classroom. For reasons which may relate to the continued presence of English as a testing medium at GCSE, many students embarking on 'A' level courses are still unprepared for this. However, the examination boards, strongly supported by SEAC, are moving decisively towards testing in the language, and this should have a significant wash-back effect on classroom practice. Whilst nearly all work is now likely to be done in the foreign language, teachers need to establish their own ground-rules concerning the borderline between $L_1$ and $L_2$, and it is important that these rules are known, understood and agreed from the start of the course.

*Student autonomy*

The style of learning required of students by the new 'A' level syllabuses is much less teacher-centred than hitherto. One only has to glance at some of the exemplar material in later chapters to see that there is a greater onus on the students to develop independent learning skills. This is as true for the preparation of texts and vocabulary acquisition as it is for small-group and pair-work activities in the classroom. Added to this, most new syllabuses contain an element of coursework, whether compulsory or optional. Currently, this means a piece or pieces of extended writing to be completed at a certain stage of the course. In the future, coursework may well be extended to cover some or all of the other skills. Some syllabuses already carry a requirement for students to make oral presentations on a prepared topic. All these practices imply a significant change in the role of the teacher, as well as new methods of working for the student. The latter may have greater freedom of choice and control over what he or she is studying; this in turn is likely to lead to improved motivation and allows the student to develop skills in an almost unlimited way. The teacher will have to learn how to manage situations in which students are learning independently, and this can be disorientating. Independent learning does not automatically lead to enhanced performance, so considerable skill is needed on the part of the teacher to ensure that there is a sense of direction, purpose and progress.

If we are to deliver an effective course which takes account of all these aspects and prepares students properly for 'A' level, it is essential that we think out clearly our objectives and plan a programme which supports the objectives and ensures that they are reached over a two-year period. The examination boards are now being obliged to make much closer links between syllabus objectives and assessment, and we as teachers shall have to do the same. In the ensuing chapters I shall follow up the implications of the issues raised above and suggest practical ways of implementing a teaching programme appropriate to the new syllabuses.

The first chapter examines the main issues affecting course planning, including the objectives in terms of content and language. Each of the Chapters 2-5 follows a common format, beginning with objectives (representing the specific skills which students at this level should be developing). This is followed by a statement of the contexts appropriate to these skills. This section is concluded by comments designed to give general guidance to teachers in that area, but the bulk of the chapter comprises sample exercises relating to each of the objectives, with a brief commentary on each. A range of exercises is normally included, though variations on a particular type are sometimes excluded for reasons of space. In such cases, reference is usually made to the various other possibilities in the commentary on the exercises. Although it is acknowledged that work on a given topic will invariably take place in a mixed-skill context (see Chapter 6: *Producing an integrated unit*), Chapters 2-5 deal with individual skills since it is felt to be important that methods of developing the skills in a (more or less) linear fashion over the course are identified.

One of the main sources of input for language and ideas comes from reading, and for this reason, reading is examined first. The almost limitless possibilities for exercises based on texts is reflected in the length of this chapter, though it is understood that many of the same exercises can be used in connection with listening. The brevity of Chapter 3 (*Developing listening*) does not therefore indicate a desire to downgrade this very important skill. The productive skills of speaking and writing have been placed after the receptive skills, since normally input is required before output can be expected, with the most difficult skill of writing coming last, since it is only after work in the other skills has taken place that writing is likely to be most effective. The emergence of speaking as perhaps the most important skill at this level is referred to elsewhere.

The last two chapters (7 and 8), though brief, relate to aspects of the 'A' level course which are integral to its success. Chapter 7 (*Assessment and monitoring*) demonstrates the close link which must be made between the statement of objectives and the means of ensuring those objectives are reached, whilst Chapter 8 examines the critical resource and support issues raised by the new syllabuses.

# Chapter 1

# STRATEGIC PLANNING

Traditionally, 'A' level language courses have evolved out of an unstructured mixture of historical practice, past examination papers, teacher interest and (lastly?) student needs. In the absence of proper syllabus definition (the sum total was often contained in the list of set books for the literature paper and a brief description of the format of the examination papers), there was little else to go on. Recent syllabuses, however, have provided significant improvements in this area. Examination boards are now much more explicit about their expectations than was the case in the past. Substantial documents containing syllabus rationale, notes for the guidance of teachers, explanations of assessment methods and weighting, lists of resources and sample examination papers are usually to be found. These are supported in some cases by resource packs and conferences for teachers, allowing a welcome exchange of views and ideas between boards, teachers and examiners. It is therefore a good moment to undertake a thorough review of the 'A' level course.

However, the syllabuses are still remarkably bare in terms of definition. In particular, none of them has yet made any attempt to define the language content other than by listing possible sources for written and spoken texts, and the nearest we can get to working out the skills that are to be tested is by close examination of the assessment criteria. The latter still vary considerably in range and precision, though it has to be said that they are very helpful in one or two cases. Teachers therefore still need to exercise their judgment, based on experience and practice, in deciding what exactly must be taught.

At the planning stage, the first priority should be to establish the long-term objectives in respect of content and language. This will help to govern and inform the eventual shape and direction of the course, and to provide the skeleton on which the flesh of the skills can be built up. The first part of this chapter will deal with the issue of these objectives. The rest of the chapter will suggest possible responses to the kind of strategic issues which 'A' level language teachers frequently have to face in attempting to achieve their objectives.

## Objectives of the 'A' level course: content

There is probably a tendency to treat content as the easiest of the course components to define, since help is already given to us in the shape of the topic lists provided by the boards. These tend to be wide-ranging and give a degree of flexibility. Any development towards assignment-based learning would probably reflect the same opportunity for choice. But at the moment, the content base as defined by the boards is still remarkably sketchy. A list of topics on which essays will or may be set in the final examination does not necessarily constitute an 'A' level course, so strategies need to be developed for ensuring that such topics are covered at some stage. But the language (and skills) components of the course may well have a strong influence on the overall course design. Coherence and progression need to be achieved through a clear structure of linguistic development related to an appropriate content framework.

In determining this content framework, certain fundamental questions need to be answered:

★ How many topics should be studied?
★ In what order should they be studied?
★ How is the choice to be made?

The amount of interest generated by topics may vary considerably. There is therefore no need to stick rigidly to a particular length for every single topic. Indeed, one of the main advantages of teaching by topics is that it gives structure and a sense of progression without losing flexibility. However, if the benefits of accumulating vocabulary, language and ideas that come with in-depth study of a topic are to be properly reaped, there is a minimum period for which one would need to be studying that topic - say ten days to a fortnight. On the other hand - and this is a temptation which becomes difficult to resist - we must be careful not to err in the opposite direction and overkill the subject. In the early stages of building up resources to support a topic-based course it is easy to use any and every resource relevant to the theme which comes to hand. This leads to over-lengthening topics and the dangers of boredom and loss of perspective, as well as irrelevance. The optimum length is probably between two and four weeks.

The questions of choice and order of topics are closely related. All the new syllabuses contain a written paper with a more or less closely defined list of topics to be prepared, usually allowing some choice. These will be referred to as 'exam topics', and are usually examined in an essay paper. There might be a tendency for teachers to cling to these listed topics as the only ones which they should include in their programme, and to get started on them as soon as possible. This should be avoided at all costs, though the exam topics obviously need to be studied in rather more depth than the other topics which form the course. They also need to be fresh in the students' minds at the time of the examination, and should not be studied until the students have already made a good deal of progress linguistically beyond GCSE, to allow them to gain maximum benefit from their study. It is therefore probably unwise to study any of the exam topics in the first year of 'A' level; instead they should provide the core of work for the second-year programme. The number of exam topics selected will depend on a variety of factors:

★ Is there a requirement by the board to do a certain number of topics?
★ How many, in the interests of students, would it be **advisable** to do, to give them a reasonable choice of questions in the examination (if appropriate)?

Given the amount of time available (the work of Year 2, if necessary), it is advisable to opt for a good coverage of the topics proposed. The relative importance of the exam topics will mean that one is likely to want to devote more time to them than to earlier topics. However, it is advisable to guard against the dangers of overkill, and an absolute maximum of five weeks is recommended. Going beyond this is counterproductive for all (including the teacher!), whatever the resources available. Above all, it is essential to avoid the temptation of wanting to introduce the exam topics too early. The material generally available is likely to be quite demanding; asking students to produce work which could be useful to them in terms of examination preparation at a time when their skills are still in the process of early development is expecting too much. 'A' level syllabuses demand a good deal linguistically; the whole of the first year can safely be regarded as contributing to students' linguistic competence and as such is vitally important 'syllabus' work. It is important to impress on students that the 'content' side of the syllabus can be tackled later.

By making a distinction between exam topics and the rest, we have already begun to answer the crucial question concerning exact choice of topics and when to study them. Some (perhaps five or six) of the topics are dictated by options in the syllabus and form the greater part of the second-year programme. In any case, even if the syllabus does not stipulate precise topics for the examination, it makes sense to study second-year topics in greater detail and depth. More difficult to resolve is the question of the first-year topics. To begin with, the single most important factor in deciding the choice may be an unprincipled one: that of available resources. However, syllabus requirements and the availability of materials now make a more rational choice of topics both important and possible. It might be helpful to list some of the functions which a careful selection should serve:

- **Cover the 'non-defined' topics which recur in the examination**

None of the examination boards defines the content of its papers other than those parts of its examination which are linked specifically to the preparation of topics for certain written or spoken language components of the examination. These are almost always linked to coursework/written language (normally an essay) and/or the oral. The guidance given as to the content of the rest of the examination (i.e. generally the listening and reading components) is minimal, at best listing briefly possible sources of material (see p 20 for list of reading contexts and pp 57-8 for listening contexts).

- **Provide a balanced and varied programme to suit the needs of a range of students**

In planning a programme, it is important to view the entire two-year course as a whole. Balance and variety should exist across the two years, and where possible within each year. If written coursework forms part of the course, it is likely that this will mostly be done in the second year. Thus, subjects chosen for the first year might offer a 'taster' for possible coursework choices. Since it is likely that students will be taking a greater range of 'A' levels than in the past, the choice of topics should also reflect a greater range of themes, e.g. geography, science and technology, business and the world of commerce, sociology, the arts. This will not only enable students to make links with their other subjects, but also provide an excellent general education. Whatever the interests of the teacher - and it may be quite desirable to exploit these - it is important not to make choices solely on the basis of his or her predilections.

- **Give insight into the foreign culture**

If the programme is balanced and varied, and the source material authentic, it is probable that it will automatically give a good insight into the foreign culture. One of the main aims of the new syllabuses is to equip students with a greater understanding of France. In selecting topics, we should therefore bear in mind not only those of current interest within our own country, but those which are important to the French. We should ask ourselves the question: 'Are there any specific topics which are regularly or frequently issues in France, which may even be peculiar to that country?' This does not mean that we should ignore or undervalue students' own experience of life in their own country - indeed it is important that they be allowed to express themselves on such issues - but we should be careful to use the foreign language in realistic contexts and to enable students to see the language and the culture as inextricably linked.

- **Deal with lively, provocative and up-to-date issues**

The two previous sections both contain references to student interests; it is essential that the topics we choose are ones which will motivate and provoke them. They are much more likely to want to express themselves or to read on subjects on which they hold views. More importantly, if they can work in subjects that interest them, this will give them a powerful impetus to develop the skills they need. In an ideal world, the students would select their own topics, and in a sense they can do this by influencing our decision-making from year to year. Obtaining regular feedback on student views is therefore vital. But given that we have to make decisions about course content, we should look closely at what works and what does not, and try to include topics which do (or should) excite them: e.g. animal rights, ecology, discrimination, politics. Vitally important, too, is the capacity to exploit current affairs, whether internal or external. Students are much more likely to be gripped by last night's news from the radio or TV than they are by events which took place months or years ago. Given the ephemeral nature of some of the subjects or issues one might wish to cover - and this refers in particular to news or current affairs - it is clearly impossible to build them into the course in advance as self-contained units. It is a good idea to build some slack into the programme so that time can be spent on topical issues as and when necessary. It is easy to become so obsessed by organisation and planning that we can overlook the enjoyment and motivation deriving from spontaneous and/or topical discussion.

- **Offer progression/permit the development of skills**

If the actual choice of topics is difficult, the order in which to study them needs even greater care. This is not because there is a right or wrong order, but because maximum benefit can only be derived from their study if carefully placed in the course and directly related to the development of linguistic skills. With experience, teachers may find that certain topics offer greater scope for the development of specific skills than others. This would presumably lead to a re-arrangement of the order in future years to allow for exploitation of those skills at an appropriate point in the course. Given the different factors already referred to, it is quite a juggling act to fulfil all the functions and maintain a logical progression in terms of content. The latter may indeed by impossible to achieve. However, just as exam topics should sensibly be reserved for the second year, topics with a strong element of personal experience may be best suited to the early stages of the course, since students will tend to have more ideas on these subjects than others, can relate them to their own lives and may already have a vocabulary base from previous studies. In the end, although some topics may have lexical or informational loads that are heavier than others, any topic is only as easy or as difficult as the tasks we ask the students to achieve. Finally, there is often sense in grouping together topics which have natural affinities, e.g. health/leisure; animal rights/life in the country; TV (the media)/advertising.

## Objectives of the 'A' level course: language

### *Functional language and vocabulary*

Clearly, the linguistic objectives of the 'A' level French course are directly related to the skills and contexts within which students are required to operate. This is as true for functional language as it is for vocabulary. Implicit in the description of the skills in Chapters 2-5 is the language necessary to achieve them. The vocabulary which students need to know (actively or passively) will be governed by the topics selected for study. Where they are expected to use productive skills in demonstrating knowledge of a topic (e.g. in extended writing or speaking), they will need to know all the vocabulary commonly associated with that topic. As far as strategic planning is concerned, provided provision is made for coverage of the necessary skills and content, the appropriate language defines itself almost automatically.

Since vocabulary is nearly always mentioned by students as a major difficulty in making the transition to 'A' level, consideration of this problem may well affect planning decisions. The problem appears to have been exacerbated by the rather narrow transactional focus of much GCSE work, though at the other end 'A' level syllabuses are guilty by default: they have left the question of vocabulary completely open-ended. This has particular implications for the work which takes place at the beginning and in the early stages of the course. It is obviously necessary to build up and widen students' general vocabulary as quickly as possible, especially of a journalistic register, so that they can deal with the longer articles which they are likely to be studying. However, great care has to be taken not to overwhelm them with inappropriate or numerous texts in the first few weeks. Care is therefore necessary on two counts: in choice of texts (so that students are not suddenly thrust into long or complex texts with technical vocabulary), and in ensuring that proper 'learner training' takes place in respect of how to cope with the vocabulary problem. (See also the *Further guidelines* section of Chapter 2, pp 20-22, for comments on the role of dictionaries.)

*The treatment of grammar*

One of the most vexed questions in the shift to more modern syllabuses is that of the importance and treatment of grammar, since traditional courses tended to place the treatment of grammar in the forefront of proceedings. A regular diet of Whitmarsh sentences and prose and dictation was fed to sixth formers, with the result that they focused their attention on the minutiae of structures much more than on language which could be used for practical purposes. And because the language study was led by grammar rather than the reverse, grammar was not infrequently taught in a vacuum, devoid of any meaningful context. The major change that has come about in the new approach is essentially a reversal of this process. Language is studied in context, functionally. Grammar study and knowledge has not, of course, disappeared. On the contrary, it is alive and well, and living in all the different situations and texts which form part of the students' course. It follows from, and arises out of, language that is actually being used to communicate a message. Students do not (or should not) see it as something organically separate, to be mastered on its own, but as a means simply of establishing the patterns or ground rules which govern the language.

It follows from this that grammatical explanations should arise naturally from the topic work. That does not mean that coverage of what are deemed to be the essential elements of grammatical knowledge for students at this level should be left entirely to chance. It is the teacher's responsibility to ensure adequate coverage over the two-year period, though there is a danger of attempting to cover too much too quickly in the early stages. It is quite possible that few grammatical explanations will have been given to students in their GCSE courses. If we are to maintain their fluency rather than suddenly deflate confidence by drawing attention to every grammatical error, and by emphasising grammar at the expense of communication, it is important to strike a balance between what they are used to and what we may feel are some of the more 'academic' requirements of the 'A' level course. We do not want students to feel that what they have done before is inadequate, nor do we wish them to change their view of language as a means of communication. On the other hand, gradually they will need to be introduced to grammatical terminology and should eventually be quite at home in foreign language explanations of all the major areas of grammar. Since the teaching of grammar **in context** is paramount, it would be impossible to prescribe an order in which points should be tackled. Appendix A contains a list of grammatical structures which might be covered and which could be used as a checklist.

As far as the status of accuracy is concerned in the new syllabuses, accurate work is still credited at appropriate points. The assessment criteria for oral and written language invariably contain references to grammatical accuracy. Its weighting may vary from board to board, but it still counts. The tendency now is for inaccuracy to remain unpenalised in comprehension papers to allow proper credit for the skill which is being tested, but it would be unwise in a teaching/learning situation to encourage students to adopt a lazy attitude towards accuracy.

## Issues affecting planning

*Staffing*

In many establishments where 'A' level is taught, the teaching of the groups has always been split between two or even three staff. For the traditional 'A' level examinations this practice was part of a vicious circle; because the teaching was shared, it was easiest to split the teaching by skill or examination paper area (e.g. prose, translation, essay, literature, oral). In turn this prevented or at the very least impeded progressive, coherent planning. Time-table arrangements are such that sharing the teaching is often still a continuing necessity. With new syllabuses and their mixed-skill methodology this presents all kinds of problems, since it is no longer possible or desirable to separate the workload in this way.

There is no easy answer to this. An obvious way out, and one adopted already by many, is to split the teaching by topics. Administratively, this is the easiest solution. It makes life easy for the teachers involved, who can do their own thing irrespective of what may be going on in the other classes. But it fragments the course from the students' point of view and clearly destroys the course as a coherent and integrated programme. If we are to put the students first, only two alternatives commend themselves. Firstly, to organise the teaching so that staff take it in turns to take complete responsibility for a group in any one year, or secondly to share the teaching and spend a certain amount of time in liaison. The latter solution can work, but it requires careful planning by staff concerned on a regular basis (e.g. weekly) and meticulous recording of work done, as measured against the projected programme. The danger is that students may seek to play staff off against each other; this can only be avoided if work set is written down and a log-book kept of the work done in each class. To avoid unnecessary fragmentation and disruption, sharing arrangements of this kind can be organised so that one member of staff takes the first two classes in a week (say) and another takes the last two.

Another aspect of staffing concerns the French assistant. Unfortunately, many schools no longer have the privilege of access to a language assistant, and, when they do, the assistant's work is often principally with younger age groups. However, where 'A' level students can have access to an assistant (or friendly native speaker) on a regular basis it makes sense to integrate him/her into the course, so that the assistant's work is not seen as an activity which is disconnected from the students' main programme. If assistants can be used to provide an extra slot in the time-table, seeing students outside their normal languages class, so much the better, as this will increase contact time with the language. However, it is important that what they do is closely linked to the students' current work, without duplication. Assistants might be encouraged to develop oral activities connected with the relevant topics. They should be discouraged from the practice of devoting their regular classes to reading or writing skills, since it is more appropriate to use their strengths in the spoken language - though many assistants have a tendency to want to seek a safe haven in textual analysis. Close links with the 'main' language classes should be maintained so that assistants do not feel sidelined in any way, and they should be encouraged to feel they are making a valuable contribution by producing activities which can be banked for future use.

*Time management*

The amount of time available to teach an 'A' level subject is not generally something over which a head of department or course tutor has much control. For 'mainstream' subjects such as French the allocation is generally in the region of four to five hours per week, with an understanding that students will probably undertake about six hours' private study/homework in addition. The kind of programme recommended in this chapter and the pattern of work implicit in the rest of the book assume this level of resourcing. The integrated nature of the modern course puts a considerable onus on the student to commit time to follow-up and preparation work in a regular (generally daily) way and the need for this must be inculcated right from the beginning of the course.

Although student autonomy is a characteristic likely to be promoted by the new approach to language learning, this does not reduce the teacher's commitment in terms of time - far from it! - but it does alter the way in which the teacher uses that time. Appropriate guidance, added preparation of teaching materials, management of resources and careful monitoring of work are some of the new functions he/she will undertake. The formality of a teacher-centred French class may frequently be replaced by the apparent anarchy of individual activity. But it is no secret among teachers already used to this way of working that it can only be effective through very skilful and time-consuming background work by the teachers. Hence the notion that students can be left to work on their own - and class contact reduced accordingly - is entirely erroneous.

In some circumstances, however, teachers may find themselves in situations where their teaching time is significantly reduced. This may be for time-tabling, staffing, historical or budgetary reasons. Where this is the case, difficult decisions regarding priorities have to be taken. A reduction in the number of topics to be covered would almost certainly have to take place, although alternatively the amount of material for each topic could be reduced. As overkill is not uncommon, this may be a better solution. Some of the negative effects could be mitigated by increasing the students' homework commitment, though this cannot be pushed too far because the additional work would, in many cases, need to be corrected in class. One of the effects of squeezing the class contact time would be further to heighten the need for independent learning skills, in particular research skills and organised reading.

*Teaching mixed groups*

The need to keep a tight rein on the budget has led many establishments to combine teaching groups where the classes are relatively small. This frequently occurs in the case of 'A' and 'AS'. Some boards' syllabuses have a degree of overlap, with common papers, and are therefore designed to facilitate this practice. However, despite the theoretical common ground, the practical problems of combining groups can be considerable, since students with differing time allocations will inevitably progress at different rates. Because of this, it is a practice which should only be adopted as a last resort.

The first temptation, in planning a programme for combined 'A' and 'AS' groups, is to run two almost parallel courses, so that one provides one package ('A' level) for Mondays and Thursdays (for example) and another, entirely self-contained, separate package ('AS') for Tuesdays and Fridays. This way of organising and programming may even be compounded by having different staff teach the different packages. But to do this produces the same kind of fragmented programmes brought about by using two staff to run their own self-contained units. If 'AS' was a basic core (X hours long), with 'A' level as the extension (a further X hours long), this would be fine, provided the two were consecutive. In that way, the course could be developed in modular fashion. But that is not, at present, the case.

On another tack, keeping certain skills to certain days (some 'AS' courses do not require writing) merely makes the whole operation artificial and takes us back to the bad old days. One solution - and it is really designed to achieve the most coherent programme for all under difficult circumstances - is to treat the whole programme as though 'AS' did not exist as a separate entity, to ignore the fact that for half the time only half the students will be present, to plan and deliver a coherent programme for 'A' level, and let the 'AS' students fit in for half the time, doing half the classwork and the relevant homework for the days when they are going to be present. To enable this to happen requires the teacher to organise the work at least a week in advance, producing a statement for each week of the work to be done in class and the work to be done for homework. 'A' level students will do everything, 'AS' students will do the classwork on the days they attend, and the bottom line for homework is that they will do all the work set for days when they attend (irrespective of the day when it was set). A sample *programme de travail* for one 'A' level group for one week is set out on p 13. All the work ringed will be done by 'AS' students, assuming they attend on Tuesday and Friday. This approach has the following advantages:

★ there is no real differentiation between 'A' and 'AS' groups in terms of the type/level of work they do;
★ there is no disruption to the 'A' level course;
★ there is no confusion as to who does what.

Problems of an entirely different kind occur where teaching groups contain a mix of students, some first year, some second year. Such situations - most commonly found in 'minority' languages - are a nightmare to handle, but can be the only way to ensure the subject survives. The way in which the problems can be resolved will depend to a significant degree on the amount of class contact time available. Let us assume this is about 'average' (i.e. four to five hours per week, divided into four classes), though one would hope the figure might be a little higher to compensate for the difficulties. Inevitably, any solutions or suggestions are bound to represent a compromise, but certain principles seem to make sense. Each group of students could have one class per week devoted to them, during which the other group has a specific task. The work undertaken by the first-year group would focus on such aspects as basic language skills, learner training, consolidation of grammatical knowledge, whilst the second-year group would deal with coursework, extension of topics for examination purposes, more difficult tasks associated with the examination, etc. For the two remaining classes, the groups would be taught together, covering the same texts and generally undertaking mixed-skill work in common. However, to cater for the different capacities of the students, the work required of them - particularly in terms of preparation and exercises based on texts - could be differentiated where appropriate. First-year students might be expected only to do selected exercises, whilst the second-year group should be able to cope with all of them. And while the second years are carrying out extended writing or more complex linguistic exercises, the first years could be spending a proportionately greater time on preparation and vocabulary acquisition.

Programme de travail pour 'A'/'AS', première année, la semaine du 24 Septembre

| JOUR | TRAVAIL A FAIRE EN CLASSE | DEVOIRS |
|---|---|---|
| Lundi | (1) RC 317 Travail du vocabulaire (préparé à l'avance s.v.p.) (2) Activité orale : avantages et inconvénients du camping | Apprenez le présent du verbe pour un test (mardi) |
| Mardi | (1) Test du présent (2) A442 Travail écrit - une histoire de camping | A442 exercice 4 (mercredi) |
| Mercredi | (1) A442 - le corrigé d'ex.4 (2) A211 Activités/discussion de groupe | * A155 Préparez un spot publicitaire sur une brochure choisie (à faire dans de petits groupes; max. 30 mots écrits) (vendredi) |
| Jeudi | (1) A153 Activité orale - 'A l'agence de voyages' | |
| Vendredi | (1) A155 Faites votre publicité (5 minutes) (2) RC214 'Lieux de vacances' (3) Révision de l'imparfait | Révisez le sujet 'Que savez-vous du tourisme?' pour un test de fin de thème (mardi) Le test sera basé sur le vocabulaire et la grammaire que vous avez faits au cours du sujet |

*Exchange visits*

The increased emphasis in the new syllabuses on broader knowledge of the culture of the country, on oral skills and on use of authentic material places a far greater premium on direct contact with the country than before. Extended periods of residence on a family-to-family basis, giving students the opportunity for complete immersion in the language, are probably the ideal form of visit, but this is not always possible, and it is usually a good deal easier for schools to organise a conventional exchange which lasts, usually, for about ten days to a fortnight. In many cases a multitude of pressures exist which tie our hands when it comes to organising an exchange. But there are a number of points which should be considered in relation to the general planning.

★ **Timing**

Policy decisions in either school concerned may affect whether the exchange takes place in term-time or holiday. There is a strong case for arguing that such a visit is an integral part of the course and should, if possible, be in term-time.

★ **Programme**

If it takes place during term-time, it is important that students are seen to be working. They should have a proper programme of work, which may include visits, excursions, talks, etc but which will ensure that they are obliged to produce something at the end. One cannot be prescriptive about what this should be, but it is essential that students see their visit as part of their study and not as a holiday. It is important that most, if not all, the organised activities are related either to a part of the course already completed - following up topics studied - or to what is to come later. Conversely, the fact that an exchange is to take place may well affect the choice or timing of topics in the two-year programme. Conscious of the opening-up of the European market and its implications for employment, schools are increasingly using the exchange as an opportunity to establish work placements or shadowing. The former tend to be more enriching for students, but need to last more than a day or two. Suitable contacts may take some time to build up, and an added difficulty is that exchanges organised on a reciprocal basis will entail setting up a similar programme for the French students when they come to this country. All this can be time-consuming and have insurance implications.

★ **Resources**

The new syllabuses are highly reliant on resources. Although many if not most teachers will not have the time to write all their own teaching materials, they will be keen to add to the bank of resources which can be used by staff and students. Topics are likely to change from time to time and a wide range of materials is essential for coursework. The exchange is thus an ideal opportunity to gather materials of all kinds. For some, it may be possible to use part of the departmental budget in this way. Another suggestion is to encourage students to look out for and collect anything which could be of use for current or future topics. Enterprising students will ferret out all sorts of useful items - and can usually be prevailed upon to carry them all back! The ethos of the new syllabuses demands that students work with authentic material. Schools, however, are often unable to afford regular subscriptions to magazines. On the exchange, it will usually be possible for students to collect recent past copies in some quantity from their host families and their friends.

### ★ Preparation and follow-up

If students are to gain the maximum benefit from their exchange, they should be properly prepared for it, with perhaps a week or two before their departure devoted to this. The preparation should acquaint students with important aspects of the history and geography of the region they are to visit. Ideally, too, they should have a good idea of the exact programme they will follow and the rationale for it, and they should certainly know what is going to be required of them in terms of work or study while they are there and when they come back. It is a good idea to set a particular task for each specific visit and students should be encouraged to prepare for any technical language they might need. In the case of work placements, given the goodwill that is being extended to students, it is important that they appear well prepared. Even more than in other situations, they should have a clear idea of why they are going and what they might learn. At the very least they should have a list of items to research or a questionnaire to complete. Some schools have already set up exciting schemes in which, for example, their coursework is centred on a comparison between particular jobs in this country and abroad, necessitating a period of work-shadowing in each. Only by careful preparation and productive follow-up can term-time exchanges be fully justified and appropriate benefits acquired. If follow-up does not result in actual coursework, then it should at least result in oral, written or visual production of some kind.

*Coursework - organisation and implications*

Although coursework is likely to be developed over the coming years to encompass other skills and competencies (indeed any kind of periodic assessment is a form of coursework), its most common form is currently extended writing. This comes in a variety of different guises, according to the syllabus. Some require a single extended piece of writing in French, some call for several shorter pieces, some locate the work in the last few months, some give no particular timescale other than a deadline. Whatever the format, written coursework presents a number of issues to be resolved which may have a significant impact on course planning. Obviously the ways in which the programme is likely to be affected will depend on the specific requirements of the syllabus. The first strategic decision - where a free choice of topics is given (and this includes choices from an extensive list, which amounts to a free choice) - is whether to allow students to make individual choices or to limit or direct that choice in some way: for example, requiring all the students or groups of them to work on the same topic area. This allows careful targetting of available resources and a certain amount of class/group work on the topic as background to the coursework (normally this is quite acceptable, provided work on the actual coursework pieces is done individually). It also means that time does not have to be devoted to individual negotiation. On the other hand, some of the prime objectives of coursework are negated by this approach. Individual choice means that students can opt for subjects which interest them and this is an important motivating factor. It also leads automatically to more one-to-one contact between student and teacher both at the planning stage (again, normally an acceptable part of coursework practice) and in the follow-up. That is undoubtedly a good thing, but whether it is practical or not will depend on local circumstance and in particular on group size. One could argue that in educational terms the arguments are in favour of giving students choice and therefore an element of control over the curriculum, provided the resources can support it (and that is a significant proviso).

The second issue to be considered is that of timing. Unless the syllabus specifically requires it, it is inadvisable to begin coursework pieces before the end of the first year. Ideally, and depending on the number of pieces to be produced, coursework should be left until the second year, for reasons which will be explained in Chapter 5 (*Developing writing*). If a single, lengthy piece is the requirement, then it is most likely that a single date will be specified by the board, but where a number of pieces are required, to be completed over a long period by a particular date and left to the discretion of centres, then planning becomes more crucial. In cases where the coursework is linked directly to topics being studied by the students as part of their programme, it is obvious to link the writing-up of the coursework to the period when the topics are being studied. If, however, the choice of coursework topics is left to the individual student, then decisions need to be made by the teacher about when and how the pieces are to be written.

In order to maximise the learning progress, it makes most sense to spread the different pieces over a period of time - say two to three terms if possible. This reduces the problem of having to produce a great deal of work in a short period which can cause excessive pressure for students and staff alike. It also enables students to learn from their earlier pieces and progress. For this to be successful, clear internal deadlines have to be set. For the same reasons, students should be strongly discouraged from allowing themselves to get into a situation of failing to meet deadlines and allowing large loads to build up as final dates for completion draw near. This can lead to intolerable burdens, particularly if the student has coursework to complete in other subjects.

The pieces themselves can either be written in private study/homework time or in class. Sometimes the syllabus stipulates that one or more pieces have to be written as 'control pieces' in supervised conditions. Sometimes centres may wish to impose such conditions themselves. Given the importance of the coursework, in terms both of the assessment value and of developing other skills whilst researching the material, a 'compromise' solution is to set aside a certain amount of class time for students to prepare and write their coursework. This helps to provide time for teachers to undertake any supervisory/guidance responsibilities they may have in relation to the coursework, to concentrate students' minds on the work in hand and to give a semi-controlled context. If coursework is to be taken seriously, adequate time must be built into the programme for its completion, and this needs to be planned from the start.

*Internal/mock examinations*

Clearly, the timing and shape of mock examinations as well as the question of assessment of students' progress, part of which may be periodic tests or an end-of-year examination, will have a considerable effect on strategic planning. For detailed comments on these issues, see the relevant section in Chapter 7 (*Assessment and monitoring*).

# KEY POINTS

**Objectives of the 'A' level course: content**

- to cover appropriate number of topics prescribed by syllabus
- to cover syllabus's 'hidden agenda' of topics
- to cover 'non-defined topics'
- to provide balance and variety
- to provide insight into French culture
- to stimulate student interest
- to provide a suitable basis for linguistic/skills development
- to allow flexibility for coverage of topical issues
- to arrange topics in an appropriate sequence

**Objectives of the 'A' level course: language**

- to teach functional language appropriate to the skills/contexts defined by the syllabus
- to teach the specific vocabulary appropriate to each of the topics selected
- to teach appropriate general vocabulary
- to distinguish between active and passive vocabulary
- to teach appropriate grammatical structures/familiarise students with grammatical terminology

**Issues affecting planning**

★ Staffing
- sharing teaching is difficult in a mixed-skill setting
- splitting teaching by skill or topic is undesirable
- maintaining a coherent programme can be achieved by careful liaison
- the work of French assistants should be fully integrated into the rest of students' work
- assistants are an important part of the team

★ Time management
- four to five hours class contact, six hours homework per week is 'normal'
- integrated courses mean daily homework
- student autonomy requires careful organisation
- where class contact is less, topics can be reduced in length and students can do more homework
- development of study skills is critical

★ Teaching mixed groups
- mixed 'A'/'AS' groups are undesirable
- full integration should be attempted
- tasks/homework for 'A'/'AS' students should be clearly differentiated
- mixed first/second year groups cannot be fully integrated (some separate teaching is necessary)
- consecutive years' programmes need to be different

★ Exchange visits
- should be integral part of course, if possible
- relevant, clear programme of work is needed, with appropriate preparation and follow-up
- opportunity to gather resources
- opportunity for work placements

★ Coursework - organisation and implications
- written coursework currently most popular form
- individual choice of topics is desirable to cater for student interest
- group choice enables targetting of resources
- extended writing should be kept for Year 2
- time organisation is essential
- coursework is a valuable learning process
- 'control' pieces may be useful

★ Internal/mock examinations

- (see Chapter 7)

Chapter 2

# DEVELOPING READING

The assumption among nearly all 'A' level French students is that reading is the easiest part of their work. When the examination comes along, the common chant is 'I don't need to revise for the Reading paper. It's easy.' Such views are right in one respect, and wrong in another. If proper and careful work on reading has gone on over the whole period of the course, then revision is unnecessary, because the skills required are laborious, time-consuming and progressive. They can only be properly acquired over an extended period. But easy? Not at all. Evidence from each summer's examinations shows that performance by candidates in this area often lags behind that in other skills. In practice, the Reading paper can often be the hardest.

The objectives will therefore represent the specific skills which students at this level should be developing, and these will be followed by a statement of the reading contexts which they are likely to meet. This section will be concluded by comments designed to give general guidance to teachers in this skill area. The bulk of the chapter will comprise sample exercises relating to the first five objectives, with brief commentary on each. There are no exercise examples for the sixth (*'Coping with different text types'*) as this is fundamental to the different 'contexts' referred to below (p 20).

**Objectives**

- ★ understanding and extending vocabulary and idiom (R1)
- ★ understanding general message (skimming) (R2)
- ★ understanding precise message (R3)
- ★ inferring meaning/understanding implications (R4)
- ★ acquiring grammatical and syntactical knowledge (grammatical structures, sentence patterns, etc) (R5)
- ★ coping with different text types

Although the balance may change from one board's requirements to another, these are the main reading skills students will need at 'A' level. Acquiring these skills is a gradual process. Some are quite demanding and are likely to take much longer to develop than others. All will need consolidating. A single exercise devoted to one of these skills will not bear much fruit. (NB: The numbers in brackets enable easy reference to these objectives, e.g. see pp 122-3, *Buts: capacités*.)

**Contexts**

Additionally, consideration needs to be given to the sources of written material, since there is a danger with 'A' level syllabuses of limiting students' experiences to a very dry form of journalistic register. Again, balance and emphasis will vary, but all students on an 'A' level course should, at some stage, have access to and be able to cope with material drawn from the following sources:

- ★ educational books written in the FL, on appropriate topics and appropriately presented
- ★ newspapers, magazines, journals
- ★ selected literary works
- ★ advertising material
- ★ leaflets, instructions designed for the public (i.e. non-specialist)
- ★ formal and informal letters

For those students for whom it is thought to be inappropriate to study full-length literary texts, extracts or pieces written in a literary register should nonetheless be introduced at chosen moments to enhance the study of their topics from both a linguistic and cultural viewpoint. Good examples of the use of such texts can be found in *Actuellement*.

**Further guidelines**

*Selection of texts*

In their GCSE work, students will already have been exposed to 'authentic' material of the kind they are likely to come across in everyday situations abroad. On the whole, they do not, therefore, have difficulty in coping with brief news articles of the *faits divers* kind, advertisements, announcements, brochures and leaflets. However, they immediately have difficulty with longer articles containing argument and analysis. Much of the problem lies with our failure to deal with reading as a skill which needs careful structuring and nurturing. It is a developmental process which takes a great deal of time in our mother tongue, but which we often leave to chance when it comes to teaching students of a foreign language. The important thing is to select with great care the texts we ask our students to read over the first couple of terms of the course and to establish precisely what skills need to be developed and at what stage. Particularly critical are the first texts placed before students as they begin their 'A' level course, since attitudes and patterns will be established which will affect their approach to their work over the whole course, whatever its duration. The prime objective will be to make students feel comfortable in what they are doing. Undue stress or confusion can easily lead them to adopt negative attitudes or give up. Early texts should seek to emphasise to students what they **do** know rather than reinforce the idea that there is a great deal they do **not** know. And the exercises should bring this out.

As a general rule, it is more effective to exploit fully a limited number of texts than to expose students to a quantity of texts with only a few exercises on each.

*The role and use of dictionaries*

Fundamental to the development of reading skills is advice and proper training in the use of a dictionary. Resource considerations may be the principal factor in deciding the type of dictionary used. But the philosophy of the new syllabus implies that all students at this level should have access to, and be trained in the use of, monolingual dictionaries. Bilingual dictionaries, on the other hand, encourage a certain amount of laziness and perpetuate the 'translation mentality' approach to language learning. 'Being' in the language is not promoted by thinking in the mother tongue. Realistically, there will be occasions when students need access to bilingual dictionaries, but they should be discouraged from using them as a constant prop. Consequently, they will need advice right at the beginning of the course on the extent of dictionary use, particularly during homework, when the temptation will be to look up every word. In order to consolidate acquisition of vocabulary, regular testing should be carried out, but as far as possible this should be done without recourse to the mother tongue, and vocabulary should only be tested which has arisen from students' work. Short, focused testing is likely to be more helpful. But whether dictionaries are prescribed or not, many students will have access to/be encouraged to use both kinds of dictionary. Exercises should therefore be developed to help students in all aspects of their use. At some stage, it will be necessary to cover all or most of the following aspects:

**BILINGUAL**

- ★ when to use the dictionary/when not to
- ★ use of abbreviations and symbols
- ★ parts of speech
- ★ how to deal with expressions/phrases
- ★ how to select the right word from several given
- ★ cross-referencing between English and French sections
- ★ finding out what other information is in the dictionary

**MONOLINGUAL (additionally)**

- ★ identifying main differences between monolingual and bilingual dictionary
- ★ identifying purposes for which monolingual dictionary can be used
- ★ understanding definitions
- ★ use of synonyms
- ★ use of monolingual dictionary to re-phrase expressions/explain

*Importance of preparation*

Whatever exercises we set on texts, and however well they are structured, thorough preparation of texts and careful reading by students is needed if full benefit is to be derived. Techniques for highlighting useful language - and ideas - should be encouraged. The importance of preparation homework cannot be exaggerated. There is a tendency for students to by-pass it.

**Study skills and language learning activities**

| DEGREE OF SUPPORT/INDEPENDENCE | RECEPTIVE PROCESS | ACTIVE TASKS |
|---|---|---|
| I WORKING WITHIN THE TEXT<br><br>Discovering the text<br><br>Collecting language/ideas | e.g. - decoding<br>- recognising<br>- identifying<br>- selecting<br>- classifying<br>- sequencing | e.g. - transcribing<br>- completing<br>- note-taking<br>- making lists of language and facts<br>- asking/answering questions |
| II WORKING AROUND THE TEXT<br><br>Sorting, practising language/ideas | e.g. - matching<br>- reorganising<br>- inferring<br>- interpreting<br>- selecting/rejecting | e.g. - summarising<br>- renarrating<br>- expanding condensed material<br>- elucidating<br>- interpreting |
| III WORKING AWAY FROM THE TEXT<br><br>Independent, integrated use of newly and previously acquired language/ideas/knowledge | | e.g. - role-playing<br>- dramatising<br>- adapting<br>- 'remaniement'<br>- counter-argument<br>- personal/imaginative writing |
| AT ALL STAGES: CROSS REFERENCE TO OTHER SOURCES & MATERIALS<br>e.g. dictionary, reference books, teacher, tape | | |

From *French 16-19: a new perspective* (Hodder & Stoughton, 1981)

*Order of exercises*

Where teachers are writing their own exercises on a text, they would do well to follow the advice on threefold exploitation in *French 16-19: a new perspective* with initial exercises on 'discovery of the text' (vocabulary, comprehension), followed by 'sorting and practising' (linguistic) and finally 'productive' exercises using language and ideas acquired (see extract below).

*Marking*

Although formal marking of the many reading exercises may not take place, class correction and monitoring are vital ingredients of the process. For detailed comments see Chapter 7.

## Developing the skills

*Understanding and extending vocabulary/idiom*

It has already been said that one of the major problems facing 'A' level students as they embark on their course is that of vocabulary. Exposure to longer and more varied texts on a range of issues brings them into contact with a huge and largely undefinable lexis. Training them to cope with this verbal onslaught is therefore a key issue.

## Exercice 1

**Regardez la page 66 du dictionnaire *Collins-Robert* et répondez aux questions suivantes dans la langue indiquée. Vous aurez besoin, pour répondre à quelques-unes des questions, de vous référer à la liste d'abbréviations du dictionnaire.**

(a) Trouvez trois exemples de chacun des suivants:

| ADJECTIFS | SUBSTANTIFS MASCULINS | SUBSTANTIFS FEMININS |
|---|---|---|

(b) Donnez le pluriel du substantif suivant:

bateau: ____________________

(c) Donnez les formes indiquées des adjectifs suivants:

| MASC. SING. | FEM. SING. | MASC. PL. | FEM. PL. |
|---|---|---|---|
| basal | ________ | ________ | ________ |
| batailleur | ________ | ________ | ________ |
| bâtard | ________ | ________ | ________ |

(d) What does the sign ~ mean?

(e) What does the dictionary tell you about the use of the expression **bas-bleu**?

(f) What does the term '(loc)' mean [see **base(e)**]?

(g) Find three examples of expressions in which words are used figuratively (in their non-literal sense) [see **base, basculer**]

(h) What is the meaning of the expression 'Et tout le bataclan'? And what is denoted by the symbol * ? [see also **bastringue**]

(i) In what kind of context is the word **bataillon** used?

(j) How many broad uses does the word **bascule** have?

(k) By looking at the meaning and use of several verbs, can you explain the differences between the symbol 'vt' after some, and 'vi' after others?

(l) Give three examples of words which can be used with **basané** to mean 'suntanned'.

(m) Qu'est-ce qu'il faut faire pour trouver le sens du mot **basculant**?

(n) Quel autre mot faut-il chercher dans le dictionnaire pour trouver un autre sens du mot **bascule**?

## Ce que vous pouvez trouver dans votre dictionnaire bilingue (Exercice 1)

(*Mus*) **basse-taille** *nf, pl* **basses-tailles** bass baritone; **bas-ventre** *nm, pl* **bas-ventres** stomach, guts.

**bas**$^{2}$ [bɑ] *nm* stocking; (*de footballeur*) sock; (*de bandit masqué*) stocking mask. **~ fins** sheer stockings; **~ de nylon** nylon stockings, nylons; **~ sans couture** seamless stockings; **~ à varices** support stockings (*Brit*) *ou* hose; **~ de laine** (*lit*) woollen stockings; (*fig*) savings, nest egg (*fig*); (*péj*) **~-bleu** bluestocking.

**basal, e,** *mpl* **-aux** [bɑzal, o] *adj* basal.

**basalte** [bazalt(ə)] *nm* basalt.

**basaltique** [bazaltik] *adj* basalt(ic).

**basané, e** [bazane] *adj teint, visage [vacancier]* (sun)tanned, sunburnt (*Brit*); *[marin]* tanned, weather-beaten; *[indigène]* swarthy.

**basculant, e** [baskylɑ̃, ɑ̃t] *adj V* **benne**.

**bascule** [baskyl] *nf* **(a)** (*balance*) *[marchandises]* weighing machine. *[personne]* **~ (automatique)** scales *(pl)*; *V* **pont**.

**(b)** (*balançoire*) (**jeu de**) **~** seesaw; **cheval/fauteuil à ~** rocking horse/chair; **faire tomber qn/qch par un mouvement de ~** to topple sb/sth over; **pratiquer une politique de ~** to have a policy of maintaining the balance of power.

**(c)** (*mécanisme*) bascule. (*Ordin*) **~ (bistable)** flip-flop.

**(d)** (*Lutte*) lift-over.

**basculer** [baskyle] (1) **1** *vi [personne]* to topple *ou* fall over, overbalance; *[objet]* to fall *ou* tip over; *[benne, planche, wagon]* to tip up; *[tas]* to topple (over). **il bascula dans le vide** he toppled over the edge; (*fig, Pol*) **~ dans l'opposition** to swing *ou* go over to the opposition.

**2** *vt* (*plus gén* **faire ~**) *benne* to tip up; *contenu* to tip out; *personne* to knock off balance, topple over.

**basculeur** [baskylœʀ] *nm* **(a)** (*Élec*) rocker switch. **(b)** (*benne*) tipper.

**base** [bɑz] **1** *nf* **(a)** *[bâtiment, colonne, triangle]* base; *[montagne]* base, foot; (*Anat, Chim, Math*) base; (*Ling: racine*) root. (*Ordin*) **~ 2/10** base 2/10.

**(b)** (*Mil etc: lieu*) base. **~ navale/aérienne** naval/air base; **rentrer à sa** *ou* **la ~** to return to base.

**(c)** (*Pol*) **la ~** the rank and file, the grass roots.

**(d)** (*principe fondamental*) basis. **~s** basis, foundations; **~s d'un traité/accord** basis of a treaty/an agreement; **raisonnement fondé sur des ~s solides** solidly-based argument; **il a des ~s solides en anglais** he has a good grounding in English *ou* a sound basic knowledge of English; **saper/renverser les ~s de...** to undermine/destroy the foundations of...; **établir** *ou* **jeter** *ou* **poser les ~s de...** to lay the foundations of... .

**(e)** (*loc*) **à ~ de: un produit à ~ de soude** a soda-based product; **être à la ~ de** to be at the root of; **sur la ~ de ces renseignements** on the basis of this information; **de ~** *prix, modèle, règles* basic; **le français de ~** basic French; (*Ling*) **forme de ~** base form; **camp de ~** base camp.

**baste**†† [bast] *excl* (*indifférence*) never mind!, who cares?; (*dédain*) pooh!

**bastide** [bastid] *nf* **(a)** (country) house (*in Provence*). **(b)** (*Hist*) walled town (*in S.W. France*).

**bastille** [bastij] *nf* fortress, castle. (*Hist*) **la B~** the Bastille.

**bastingage** [bastɛ̃gaʒ] *nm* (*Naut*) (ship's) rail; (*Hist*) bulwark.

**bastion** [bastjɔ̃] *nm* bastion; (*fig*) bastion, stronghold.

**bastonnade**†† [bastɔnad] *nf* drubbing, beating.

**bastringue*** [bastʀɛ̃g] *nm* **(a)** (*objets*) junk*, clobber‡ (*Brit*). **et tout le ~** the whole caboodle (*Brit*) *ou* kit and caboodle (*US*). **(b)** (*bruit*) racket*, din*. **(c)** (*bal*) (local) dance hall; (*orchestre*) band.

**Basutoland** [basytɔlɑ̃d] *nm* Basutoland.

**bat** *abrév de* **bâtiment**.

**bât** [bɑ] *nm* packsaddle. (*fig*) **c'est là où le ~ blesse** that's where the shoe pinches.

**bataclan*** [bataklɑ̃] *nm* junk*, clobber‡ (*Brit*). **...et tout le ~** ...and everything else, ...the whole kit and caboodle (*US*), ...and what have you*.

**bataille** [bataj] **1** *nf* **(a)** (*Mil*) battle; (*rixe*) fight; (*fig*) fight, struggle; (*controverse*) fight, dispute. **~ de rue** street fight *ou* battle; **la vie est une dure ~** life is a hard fight *ou* struggle.

**(b)** (*Cartes*) beggar-my-neighbour.

**(c)** (*loc*) **en ~** (*Mil, Naut*) in battle order *ou* formation; **il a les cheveux en ~** his hair's all dishevelled *ou* tousled; **le chapeau en ~** with his hat on askew; **être garé en ~** to be parked at an angle to the kerb.

**2**: **bataille aérienne** air battle; **bataille de boules de neige** snowball fight; **bataille électorale** election; **bataille navale** naval battle; **bataille rangée** pitched battle.

**batailler** [bataje] (1) *vi* (*fig: lutter*) to fight, battle.

**batailleur, -euse** [batajœʀ, øz] **1** *adj* pugnacious, aggressive. **il est ~** he loves a fight. **2** *nm,f* fighter (*fig*).

**bataillon** [batajɔ̃] *nm* (*Mil*) battalion; (*fig*) crowd, herd.

**bâtard, e** [bɑtaʀ, aʀd(e)] **1** *adj enfant* illegitimate, bastard† (*péj, épith*); (*fig*) *œuvre, solution* hybrid (*épith*). **chien ~** mongrel. **2** *nm,f* (*personne*) illegitimate child, bastard† (*péj*); (*chien*) mongrel. **3** *nm* (*Boulangerie*) ≃ Vienna roll. **4 bâtarde** *nf* (*Typ*: *aussi* **écriture ~e**) slanting round-hand.

**bâtardise** [bɑtaʀdiz] *nf* bastardy† (*péj*), illegitimacy.

**batavia** [batavja] *nf* Webb lettuce.

**bateau,** *pl* **~x** [bato] **1** *nm* **(a)** (*gén*) boat; (*grand*) ship. **~ à moteur/à rames/à voiles** motor/rowing/sailing boat; **prendre le ~** (*embarquer*) to embark, take the boat (*à* at); (*voyager*) to go by boat, sail; **aller en ~** to go by boat, sail; **faire du ~** (*à voiles*) to go sailing; (*à rames etc*) to go boating.

**(b)** *[trottoir]* driveway entrance (*depression in kerb*).

**2** *adj inv* (‡: *banal*) hackneyed. **c'est (un sujet** *ou* **thème) ~** it's the same old theme* *ou* the favourite topic (that crops up every

## Ce que vous pouvez trouver dans votre dictionnaire monolingue (Exercice 2)

2. BAS. *n. m.* • 1° Vêtement souple qui sert à couvrir le pied et la jambe. *Bas de laine. Bas court.* V. **Chaussette, mi-bas.** — Vêtement féminin qui couvre le pied et la jambe jusqu'au haut des cuisses. *Bas de nylon. Bas sans couture.* • 2° *Bas de laine*, argent économisé, petite épargne (d'après la coutume de garder ses économies dans un bas de laine).

BASALTE [bazalt(ə)]. *n. m.* • Roche éruptive dont la pâte compacte et noire est formée de cristaux. *Une coulée de basalte.* ▼ BASALTIQUE. *adj.* Formé de basalte.

BASANE [bazan]. *n. f.* • Peau de mouton tannée. *Livre relié en basane.* — Peau très souple garnissant un pantalon de cavalier.

BASANÉ, ÉE [bazane]. *adj.* • Se dit d'une peau brunie. V. **Bistré, tanné.** *Un visage basané.*

BAS-BLEU [bɑblø]. *n. m.* • Femme à prétentions littéraires. V. **Pédante.** *Des bas-bleus.*

BAS-CÔTÉ [bakote]. *n. m.* • 1° Nef latérale d'une église dont la voûte est moins élevée que la nef principale. • 2° Côté d'une voie, où les piétons peuvent marcher.

BASCULE [baskyl]. *n. f.* • 1° Pièce ou machine mobile sur un pivot et dont on fait lever une extrémité en abaissant l'autre. — *Jeu de bascule*, jeu où deux personnes, assises chacune sur le bout d'une pièce de bois en équilibre sur un pivot, s'amusent à se balancer. V. **Balançoire.** • 2° Alternance de mouvements en sens contraire. *Politique de bascule*, système qui consiste à s'appuyer alternativement sur deux partis opposés. • 3° *Balance à bascule* ou *Bascule*, appareil à plate-forme qui sert à peser les objets lourds, les personnes. *La bascule du pharmacien.* ▼ BASCULER. *v.* (1) • 1° *V. intr.* Faire un mouvement de bascule. V. **Culbuter.** *Une benne qui peut basculer* (benne *basculante*). • 2° *V. tr.* Faire faire un mouvement de bascule à (qqn, qqch.). • 3° *V. intr.* Passer brusquement dans. *Basculer dans l'opposition.*

BASE [bɑz]. *n. f.* ★ I. • 1° Partie inférieure

**fond, source.** *Les bases d'une science. Donnée qui sert de base à un calcul. Être à la base de qqch.*, à l'origine, à la source. — *Salaire de base*, le plus bas, qui sert de référence. — *Les militants de base*, ceux qui n'ont pas de responsabilités dans un parti ou un syndicat (par oppos. à l'appareil, aux dirigeants). *La base*, l'ensemble de ces militants. ▼ BASER. *v. tr.* (1) ★ I. *(Abstrait).* Faire reposer sur (telle ou telle base). *Les faits sur lesquels il base sa théorie.* V. **Fonder.** — SE BASER : s'appuyer. *Sur quoi vous basez-vous pour affirmer cela ?* ★ II. *Être basé quelque part*, avoir pour base (militaire).

BASE-BALL [bɛzbol]. *n. m.* • Jeu de balle dérivé du cricket, pratiqué aux États-Unis.

BAS-FOND [bɑfɔ̃]. *n. m.* • 1° Partie du fond de la mer, d'un fleuve, où l'eau est peu profonde. V. **Haut-fond.** • 2° Terrain bas et enfoncé. *Un bas-fond marécageux.* • 3° *Au plur.* Couches misérables de la société où l'homme se dégrade. *Les bas-fonds d'une grande ville.*

1. BASILIC [bazilik]. *n. m.* • Grand lézard d'Amérique, à crête dorsale, voisin de l'iguane.

2. BASILIC. *n. m.* • Plante à feuilles aromatiques employée comme condiment.

BASILIQUE [bazilik]. *n. f.* • Église chrétienne du moyen âge divisée en nefs parallèles. — Appellation de certains sanctuaires. *La basilique de Lourdes.*

BASKET-BALL [baskɛtbol] ou BASKET. *n. m.* • Jeu entre deux équipes de cinq joueurs *(basketteurs)* qui doivent lancer un ballon dans le panier du camp adverse.

BASOCHE [bazɔʃ]. *n. f.* • Vx. Les gens de justice.

1. BASQUE [bask(ə)]. *n. f.* • Partie rapportée d'une veste qui part de la taille et descend plus ou moins bas sur les hanches. *Les basques d'une jaquette.* — Loc. *Être toujours pendu aux basques de qqn*, ne pas le quitter d'un pas.

## Exercice 2

**(a) Regardez la page 93 du dictionnaire *Micro-Robert* et dites, oui ou non, si vous pouvez trouver les renseignements suivants dans ce dictionnaire monolingue:**

| | | OUI | NON |
|---|---|---|---|
| (1) | Comment prononcer les mots. | | |
| (2) | Le genre des substantifs. | | |
| (3) | Les pluriels réguliers des adjectifs. | | |
| (4) | Si les mots/expressions sont péjoratifs. | | |
| (5) | Les contextes dans lesquels les mots sont employés (p.ex. Historique, Géographique, Militaire etc) | | |
| (6) | Si un mot est employé dans des locutions. | | |
| (7) | Des synonymes pour un mot. | | |
| (8) | Des mots avec le sens contraire. | | |

**(b) Comparez la définition donnée dans les deux dictionnaires pour le mot 'bas'.**

- Quelle est la différence?
- Quel dictionnaire est le plus utile pour vous, en tant qu'étudiant de langues?
- Lequel est le plus facile à lire?
- Lequel donne le plus de renseignements?

**(c) Cherchez dans le dictionnaire le sens des expressions suivantes, et expliquez-les *en vos propres termes*, sans copier les définitions données:**

- être toujours pendu aux basques de quelqu'un
- les bas-fonds d'une grande ville

***Exercises 1 and 2** relate specifically to the use of the Collins-Robert bilingual and Micro-Robert monolingual dictionaries (parts of the relevant pages are reproduced here). Essentially, the exercises guide students to find out what kind of information the dictionaries contain, and therefore alert them to the potential of the dictionary as a learning tool.*

## Exercice 3 - Les réseaux de mots

**Regardez les exemples de 'réseaux de mots' ci-dessous. Ces réseaux sont des façons utiles de noter et de vous rappeler**

**(a) les mots associés à un sujet**
**(b) les mots de la même famille**

**EXEMPLE A (mots associés):**

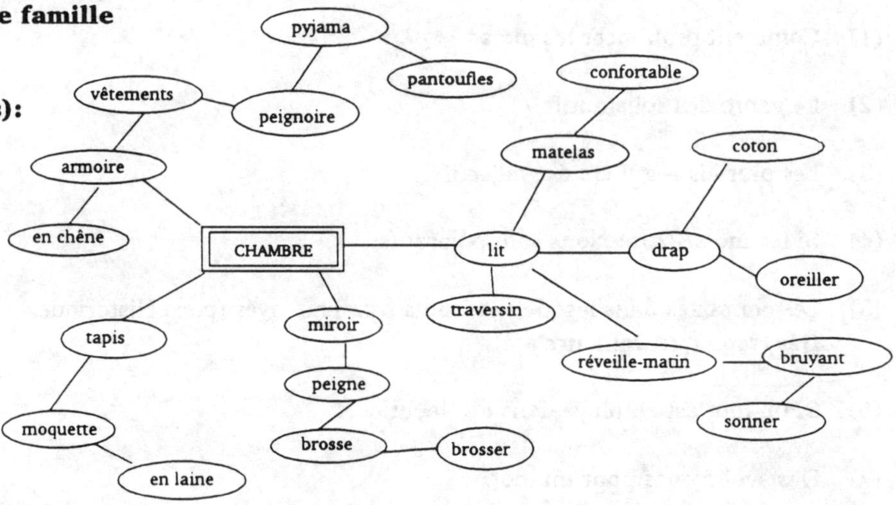


**EXEMPLE B (mots de la même famille):**

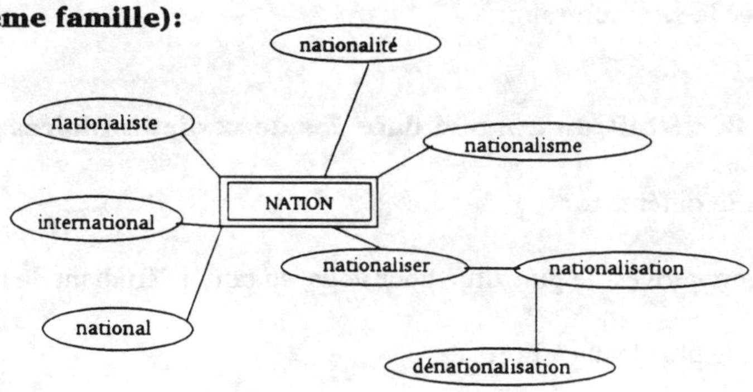


**Maintenant, regardez un texte que vous avez étudié récemment et choisissez un mot que vous jugez important dans le texte. Ecrivez-le au milieu d'une feuille blanche. Etablissez un 'réseau de mots', ajoutant des mots qui sont reliés au premier mot. Ces mots peuvent être des mots qui sont aussi dans le texte, que vous connaissez déjà, ou que vous allez trouver dans le dictionnaire.**

**Cette stratégie est une bonne façon d'augmenter votre vocabulaire. Testez-vous plus tard. Vous serez probablement surpris du nombre de mots que vous vous rappellerez. Gardez les réseaux dans votre dossier, et ajoutez des mots de temps en temps.**

***Exercise 3*** *is an example of how vocabulary can be extended through 'word networks'. Students are encouraged to build them up from texts or topics. Variations can include getting them to identify genders, or build up networks concentrating on an individual part of speech.*

## Exercice 4

*L'Etranger, Deuxième partie, Chapitre 2*

**Voici une liste de quelques-uns des mots qui figurent dans ce chapitre, dans l'ordre où ils apparaissent dans le texte. A la fin, vous trouverez les définitions qui appartiennent à ces mots tels qu'ils sont employés dans ce contexte précis - mais dans le désordre. Cherchez chaque mot dans le texte, trouvez la bonne définition dans la liste donnée, et écrivez-la dans l'espace donnée.**

| MOT | DEFINITION |
|---|---|
| un détenu | ______________________ |
| un traversin | ______________________ |
| une cuvette | ______________________ |
| éclairée | ______________________ |
| cru(e) | ______________________ |
| l'étourdissement | ______________________ |
| s'accroupir | ______________________ |
| parvenir à | ______________________ |

DEFINITIONS

1 illuminée
2 quelqu'un qui est incarcéré (dans une prison)
3 oreiller long sur lequel on repose la tête, dans un lit
4 s'asseoir sur ses talons
5 trouble qui fait que tout semble tourner; vertige
6 réussir à
7 bassin métallique ou de faience, servant à laver ou à se laver
8 violent(e)

***Exercise 4*** *has a number of functions. Often, it is set to be done before the reading of the text to familiarise students with vocabulary they may not know. Additionally, it teaches them awareness of different parts of speech (infinitives are always defined by another infinitive at the beginning of the definition, etc), and this in turn shows them how to define certain types of word (quelqu'un qui ... etc). As a test, this exercise can be set in reverse, with the definitions given and students having to name the word defined. A variation of this exercise is to ask students to find equivalent words or phrases in the text. This can be done by giving an English translation or French synonyms. Both these can be extremely tricky unless the phrases are reasonably long (several words at least) or the section of the text is clearly identified. Another variation is simply to identify difficult words and ask students to research their meaning and be prepared to explain them.*

## Exercice 5

*Travail oral et écrit à deux*

# UN TUNNEL SOUS LA MEIJE

## ...OU LES NOUVEAUX IMPOTS HYDRONUCLEAIRES SUR LE PATRIMOINE

***400 milliards de centimes : voilà ce que risque de coûter une entreprise d'une envergure folle, folle, folle... Deux barrages EDF au pied de la Meije, dans les Hautes-Alpes. Cela se passerait dans la vallée de la Haute-Romanche, près du Parc National des Ecrins. Et la Meije est un bijou de notre patrimoine national. Alors, pourquoi cet impôt sur le patrimoine ?***

Travaux gigantesques, mais pour demain : l'enquête d'utilité publique n'est annoncée que pour 1984. Question largement d'actualité puisque EDF a déjà engagé des travaux dès la fin de l'été 1981, pour des reconnaissances de terrain. Le terrain ne semble pas reconnaissant, et en tout cas pas les habitants du pays de la Meije... Pensez donc, on prévoit notamment le creusement d'une galerie d'accès au futur barrage du Plan de l'Alpe... Coût de l'opération : 20 millions de francs. Cela nécessiterait le creusement de 20 kilomètres de galeries de 4 à 7 mètres de diamètre. Un véritable tunnel sous la Meije ! Dans le tableau, deux usines, au-dessous et au-dessus du Plan de l'Alpe : au Lautaret et au Cuculet (avec une variante au Parizet). Ce barrage n'aurait *que* 100 mètres de hauteur. C'est en effet peu, si l'on songe à celui qui serait édifié dans le cirque de Goléon : 140 m...

Certes, la montagne est menacée, mais il faut bien produire cette électricité qui permet à vos journaux, si écologiques soient-ils, de sortir... Attention ! Redisons-le : il ne s'agit pas de simples barrages hydroélectriques. Le débit d'eau de la Romanche et du Maurian est trop faible. Il s'agit ici du « transfert d'énergie par pompage ». Les critères actuellement retenus pour la recherche d'un site sont d'une part sa « capacité à constituer un bon réservoir de stockage », d'autre part « la hauteur de chute possible » (voir schéma ci-contre). Il y a donc le processus aller (flèche noire) : l'eau est pompée avec l'énergie d'origine nucléaire quand on ne sait pas qu'en faire.

**Ce texte est riche en adjectifs. Ci-dessous vous trouverez (à gauche) une liste de substantifs. A vous de trouver l'adjectif dans la liste à droite qui est utilisé dans le texte pour le décrire. Ne trichez pas en regardant le texte! L'accord des adjectifs est déjà une indication!**

| | | | |
|---|---|---|---|
| travaux | ______ | A | technologiques |
| barrages | ______ | B | locale |
| centrales | ______ | C | naturelle |
| inconvénients | ______ | D | nucléaires |
| violences | ______ | E | gigantesques |
| nuisances | ______ | F | climatiques |
| trafic | ______ | G | périphériques |
| sondages | ______ | H | insoupçonnables |
| massifs | ______ | I | sismiques |
| fréquentation | ______ | J | hydroélectriques |
| vie | ______ | K | routier |
| avis | ______ | L | immergées |
| zone | ______ | M | glaciaires |
| réserve | ______ | N | partielle |
| destruction | ______ | O | touristique |
| perturbations | ______ | P | graves |
| vallées | ______ | Q | défavorable |

***Exercise 5** can only be done once the reader is familiar with the text. At one level, it could be done as a grammatical exercise, since clearly only certain adjectives demonstrate the correct agreement. Its main intention is to reinforce word-groupings and therefore certain ideas/concepts. An additional exercise can be to get students to remember the original context in which each phrase was used.*

## Exercice 6

**Travail de vocabulaire, qui vous aidera à deviner le sens des mots, sans utiliser tout le temps le dictionnaire.**

# LE LOUVRE AUJOURD'HUI

Au cœur d'une capitale, aux croisements des secousses historiques, et aujourd'hui au centre d'un renouveau culturel et architectural, le Louvre est inscrit dans les grandes réalisations qui président à la mémoire d'une nation. Mais qu'est-ce que le Louvre? Un bâtiment, une suite de longs couloirs, un ensemble de collections prestigieuses... ou déjà une nouvelle approche de l'art et de son histoire? Depuis le début de la décennie 1980, les doutes et les certitudes concernant ce qu'il devait être n'ont pas manqué de se manifester, parfois de façon polémique. N'a-t-on pas parlé de « Bataille du Louvre »? Aujourd'hui que le public a accès aux salles par la pyramide, chacun peut se rendre compte des travaux accomplis et du résultat des études qui ont réuni conservateurs, architectes, artisans, techniciens et artistes. Lumière, facilités d'accès, redéploiement et meilleures conditions de visite sont au rendez-vous. Mais 1989 n'est qu'une étape. Le réaménagement n'est pas terminé, et les nouvelles façons de « vister » le Louvre se mettront progressivement en place avec le public, ses attentes, ses habitudes, ses exigences et - toujours - ses émerveillements. Le Louvre lui-même s'est rajeuni. Parmi les 1 200 personnes qui travaillent à l'intérieur de ce « monstre sacré », beaucoup viennent d'horizons et de formations différents. C'est que pour accéder au rang très convoité de grande agora parisienne, il fallait aussi que le Louvre se dotât des moyens - en techniques et en personnel - susceptibles d'attirer un public nouveau et élargi.

**(a) Donnez les renseignements indiqués.**

| Mots qui <u>ressemblent</u> aux mots anglais, avec le même sens (n'écrivez pas les mots <u>identiques</u> comme 'nation'):<br><br>p.ex. la capitale, accompli(s) | |
|---|---|

**(b) Devinez le sens des mots suivants, à cause de leur rapport ou ressemblance avec des mots que vous connaissez déjà.**

| **français** | **mot auquel il ressemble** | **anglais** |
|---|---|---|
| p.ex.<br>les croisements<br>une secousse<br>un renouveau<br>ses attentes<br>ses émerveillements<br>s'est rajeuni | <br>**une croix/croiser**<br>**secouer** | <br>**cross-roads, crossing of paths**<br>**shaking, upheaval** |

**(c) Devinez le sens des mots suivants, selon le contexte.**

| **mot** | **définition** | **synonyme** |
|---|---|---|
| une décennie<br>un couloir<br>une étape<br>le réaménagement<br>attirer | | |

*The position of **Exercise 6** last in this section is due more to its perceived than its actual difficulty. Its aim - to encourage students to use their powers of observation and their existing knowledge to work out the meaning of words for themselves - is a fundamental one in the section. In some senses, it might have been better placed at the beginning. However, it does require students to think, particularly about the context in which words occur. Question (c) is critical in this respect.*

*Understanding general message*

Nearly all the new 'A' level syllabuses quote this skill as one of the objectives of the course, usually coupled immediately with 'understanding detail'. Occasionally it is referred to as 'gist'. However, although the skill is certainly useful to linguists, it is not one to which much thought or care has been devoted; generally both writers of text books/teaching materials and setters of examination papers concentrate on understanding detail. As a result, it is quite difficult to find many different exercise types which either test or encourage the development of reading to understand gist. The common feature of exercises which do, is that they require a considerable amount of synthesis of a text or part of it. In some cases, they may require the selection of some important pieces of information, thus encouraging students to make qualitative judgments; in others, it will be a case of drawing conclusions from the text overall. Exercises which require readers to select occasional specific items are really more to do with understanding detail, and will form part of the section after this one.

## Exercice 7

Où s'arrête la menace ? Les spécialistes ne cachent pas leur inquiétude. « On peut mettre la France à genoux », constate froidement Alain Monod-Broca, directeur du GSIT (Groupe système interbancaire télécompensation). Comment ? En paralysant tout simplement son système de communication bancaire, dont le GSIT est l'un des piliers. « Or, précise Monod-Broca, nous réaliserons, en 1990, 20 millions d'opérations interbancaires par jour ! Vous attaquez EDF, la SNCF, les Télécom, le GSIT, et vous tétanisez le pays. »

On a évoqué la Mafia ; apparemment, elle est partout. Des enquêteurs américains ont avancé l'hypothèse suivante : le krach d'octobre 1987 pourrait avoir été volontairement provoqué par une attaque (par exemple, au virus) du système informatique de Wall Street. En général, l'organisation criminelle ne s'encombre pas de détails : lorsqu'elle commença à s'intéresser sérieusement aux nouvelles potentialités offertes par l'informatique pour les détournements de fonds, elle a cherché à obtenir les informations confidentielles que possédait IBM. Mais n'entre pas qui veut dans le système informatique de Big Blue. Les données sensibles étant protégées par un système d'identification digitale, il fallait montrer patte blanche : l'ordinateur avait en mémoire les empreintes des membres du personnel habilités à l'utiliser. Finis les risques de corruption ou les faiblesses sous la torture... Finis ? La Mafia kidnappa un cadre d'IBM et lui coupa l'index. Puis s'en servit, pendant une quinzaine de jours, pour pénétrer les réseaux d'IBM.

Dès le début des années 80, des collégiens et des étudiants défrayèrent la chronique en s'introduisant, par jeu et par défi, dans les arcanes interdits du Pentagone, du CEA, de l'Ecole polytechnique ou encore de la multinationale ATT. Ils firent plus de peur que de mal, mais, surtout, ils dévoilèrent une réalité jusque-là ignorée : n'importe quel informaticien un peu doué pouvait percer des systèmes de sécurité réputés inviolables. Grâce à ces jeunes « hackers », un large débat s'est ouvert... aux Etats-Unis. Mais pas en France. « En matière de sécurité informatique, nous avons de dix à quinze ans de retard », constatent unanimement les experts.

**Visualisation d'un virus informatique.**

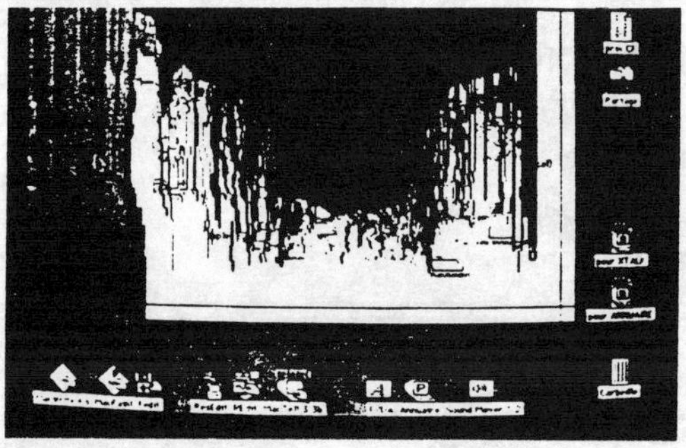

**Après avoir étudié le texte, voulez-vous inventer un titre approprié?**

***Exercise 7*** *is a very simple one, and one which can be used on almost any text. Although simple, it can lead to a good deal of debate and discussion, particularly if a number of similar ideas are generated. This will often lead on to discussion of issues such as register, appropriacy and so on. Clearly, students will need to understand most of the general information in the text, but could reach a conclusion without reference to details. Other reasonably straightforward exercises to write, and which encourage gist comprehension, are the matching of phrases to paragraphs in the text ('Mariez chacune des phrases suivantes avec le paragraphe dans le texte dont elle est le résumé') or asking the students to identify the sentence in each paragraph which best summarises its content. A more difficult variation is to get them to think of a phrase or sentence which paraphrases the main idea of each paragraph. Question and Answer in French can be a more specific way of achieving this, but the questions need to be carefully worded so that they elicit general sense rather than individual items of detail. Another alternative is to ask students to summarise the text in English, in a specific number of words - say 40/50. By limiting the length, a selection process has to take place. Summarising is a notoriously difficult exercise and many students are rightly nervous of it, because so often it is not clear whether they are actually being asked to summarise (i.e. reduce significantly the length of the stimulus passage) or merely re-phrase all the information in their own words. Where a word count is not stipulated, students are right to go for the latter approach, as marks are invariably being awarded for different points made/understood. Such an exercise clearly calls for detailed understanding.*

*Understanding precise message*

Because of the wealth of exercises developing this particular skill, it has been necessary to make a selection here, to give a good cross-section in terms of difficulty and technique. Placing the exercises in a logical or sequential order has not been easy; in one or two cases exercises have been juxtaposed because of their obvious similarity of approach, though they may be poles apart in what they demand of students. Most of the earlier exercises are less demanding in that they do not require active production of the language, though that does not necessarily make them easy as tests of comprehension. Many of the later exercises, whilst being principally tests of understanding, also require written (or spoken) language. They have nonetheless been included in this section because their main purpose is to encourage students to think about the meaning of the text. They would or could become linguistic in their bias if a proportion of the marks was allocated to accuracy. Some of the more obvious and well-known exercises have not been included since they are already in extensive use, for example '*Dites si les constatations suivantes sont vraies ou fausses*' or '*Mettez les idées suivantes dans l'ordre où ils apparaissent dans le texte*'.

## Exercice 8

**Mettez un '+' ou un '-' pour répondre à chacune des comparaisons suivantes (+ = augmentation; - = baisse).**

(a) l'électricité produite en 84 par rapport à 74 =

(b) la proportion occupée par l'énergie nucléaire en 84 par rapport à 74 =

(c) la quantité d'énergie produite par le gaz en 84 par rapport à 74 =

(d) la quantité d'énergie électrique consommée (en 1984) par rapport à la production =

(e) la consommation d'énergie à base de gaz en 1984 par rapport à la production =

**Production d'énergie** (Haute-Normandie)

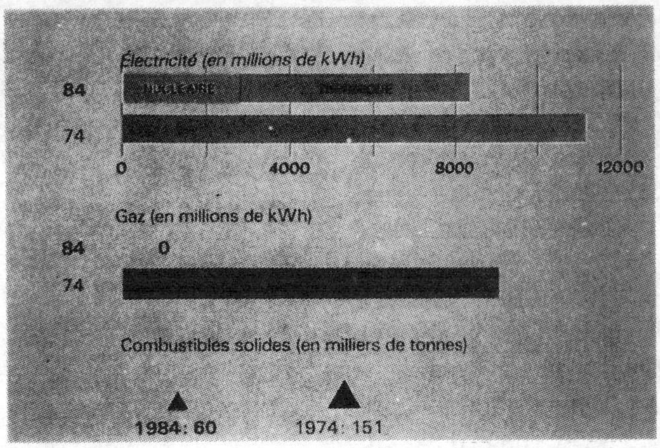


**Consommation d'énergie** (Haute-Normandie)

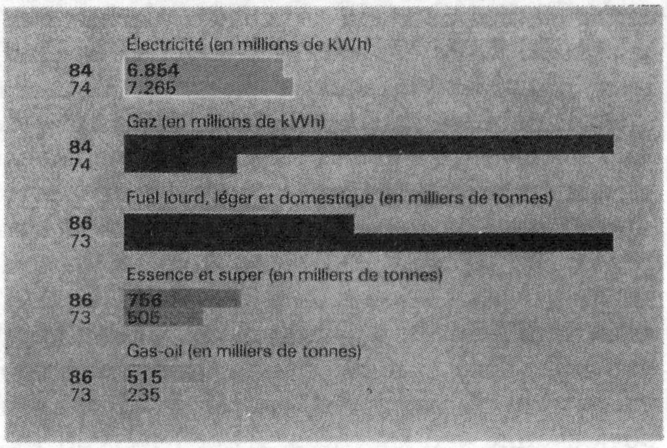


**Principaux établissements industriels** (Haute-Normandie)

| *Raison sociale* | *Commune* | *Département* |
|---|---|---|
| Renault | Sandouville | Seine-Maritime |
| Renault | Cléon | Seine-Maritime |
| Compagnie française de Raffinage | Gonfreville l'Orcher | Seine-Maritime |
| Saint-Gobain des Jonquères | Le Tréport | Seine-Maritime |
| C.D.F. Chimie Azote | Grand Quevilly | Seine-Maritime |
| S.A.G.E.M. | Saint-Étienne-du-Rouvray | Seine-Maritime |
| S.E.P. (Européenne de propulsion) | Vernon | Eure |

C. Délu-Explorer

*Plate-forme de forage pétrolier au large du Havre.*

**Commerce** (Haute- et Basse-Normandie)

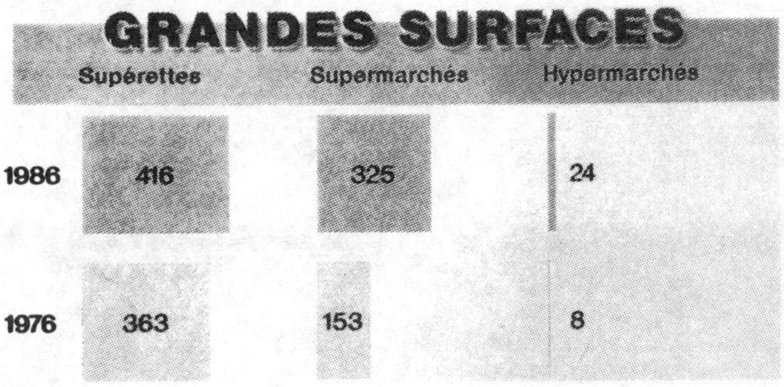


**Commerce** (Haute- et Basse-Normandie)

**Transports, tourisme et communications** (Haute- et Basse-Normandie)

Les deux régions offraient, en 1984, 2.731 places dans les maisons familiales de vacances, 3.888 chambres dans les Auberges et Logis de France et 4 482 lits dans les villages de vacances et les Auberges de Jeunesse. En outre, les crèches et pouponnières pouvaient héberger 4 145 enfants.

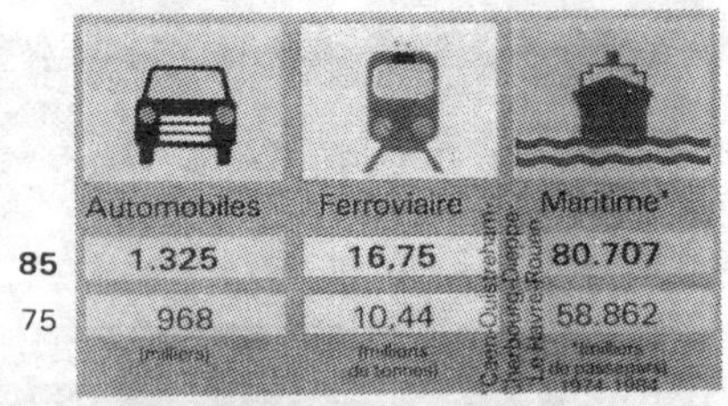


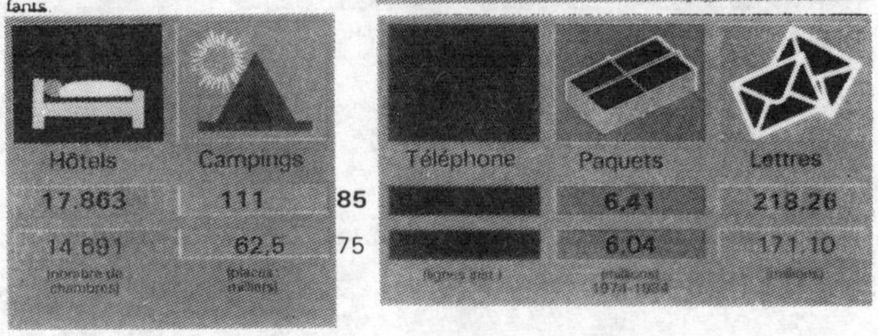

## Exercice 9

**Dessinez des graphiques pour montrer l'exploitation des sols dans les domaines indiqués pour 1985 et 1975. Le premier a déjà été fait pour vous montrer comment.**

(a) Superficie boisée (en milliers d'hectares)

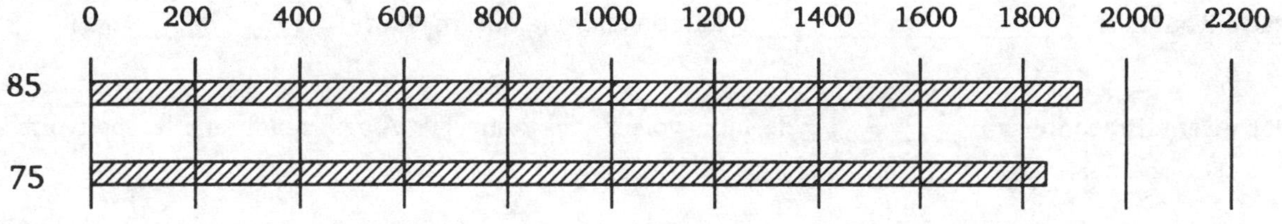


(b) Livraison de bois (milliers $m^3$)

(c) Superficie agricole (milliers ha)

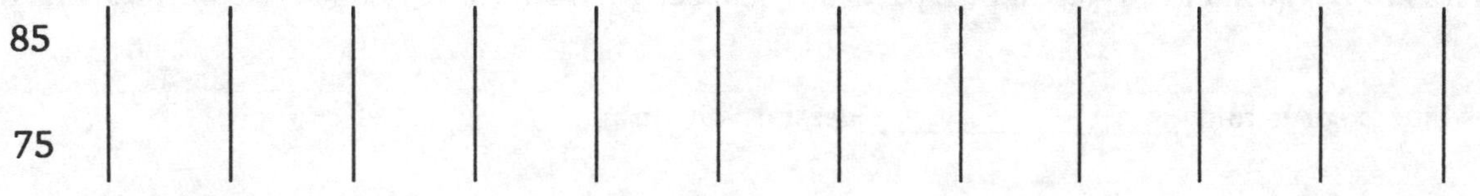


(d) Nombre d'exploitations

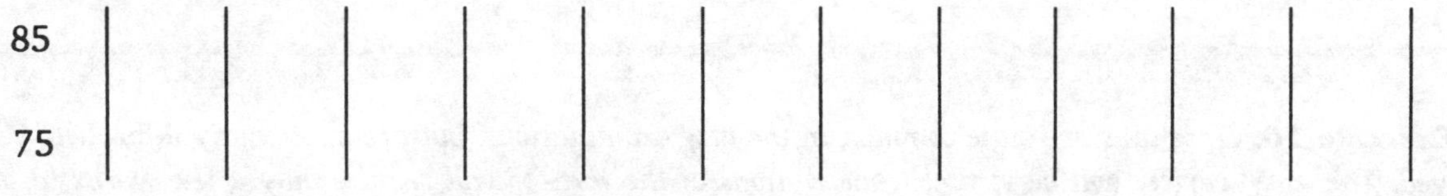


***Exercise 8** has been placed first among those developing or requiring understanding of precise message, since it demands the briefest of non-verbal responses. It is obviously appropriate and useful for students to be able to deal with numerical or statistical informatiom, whether in tabular, diagrammatical or some other form. However, although the examples given here are very straightforward, ease of answer (i.e. choices between + or -) should not necessarily be equated with ease of understanding. If the information is presented in a more complex way, or the questions are set differently, this could prove a more demanding exercise. **Exercise 9** is a further example of non-verbal responses and again is linked to statistical information. Such exercises are, of course, pure tests of comprehension.*

## ▼ Exercice 10

**Sans regarder le texte, remplissez les blancs dans la section du texte ci-dessous avec l'un des mots dans la liste suivante:**

ceux en les pollueurs leur souvent des alors voire

Parfois aussi, il ____________ faut défendre la nature contre ________ qui la détruisent. Braconniers, ________ de lacs, voleurs de 'reine des Alpes, redoutent les pouvoirs de police des 'shérifs des neiges'. Tout en ________ respectant; ils comptent parmi les meilleurs skieurs et grimpeurs des Alpes, et, en cas d'avalanche, quand une cordée est ________ perdition, on sait que les gardes du Parc seront là, ____________ les premiers. Beaucoup d'entre eux sont ________ enfants du pays, ou ses fils adoptifs, comme Robert Keck l'alsacien. ____________ on les écoute, quand ils suggèrent de réparer une chapelle abandonnée et viennent eux-mêmes remettre des lauzes sur le toit, ____________ dessiner un vitrail.

***Exercise 10.*** *Cloze tests are quite common in the new examinations, but are notoriously difficult to set well. The 'easy' variety will be virtual transcriptions of the text, or will require only a few words to be found. Here, the actual words missing are provided, out of order. This particular version, a reproduction of the source text [not reproduced here], is intended more as a test piece. Slightly more difficult will be a list including some extra 'distractors'. Careful choice of passage or language is needed in the text provided as the basis for the exercise, since so often students stumble through not understanding the context around the gap. When the missing words are not provided, it is important to make the summary of the text a straightforward one which can be readily related to the original text, otherwise the hunt for words becomes an impossibility. An alternative is to construct single sentences with a gap, and give the students a choice of answers, e.g. 'Meursault a répondu qu'il trouvait son affaire très ________ (compliqué/intéressant/simple)'. It ought to be said that cloze tests require a good grasp of grammatical concepts; the right answers can as often be worked out by the grammatical context as the sense context. They can therefore be used to develop either comprehension or grammatical skills.*

## Exercice 11

# L'AGRICULTURE EN LIVRADOIS-FOREZ

## Des handicaps sérieux... et le dynamisme pour les surmonter

L'Agriculture constitue **l'activité économique essentielle** du Livradois-Forez : un actif sur quatre. Principalement orientée vers l'élevage et la production laitière, l'agriculture en Livradois-Forez doit faire face à de lourdes difficultés :

— **Des handicaps naturels**, plus particulièrement accusés dans les zones les plus montagneuses :

- — un climat rigoureux;
- — des sols acides souvent pauvres et peu profonds;
- — un relief parfois accusé.

— **Des structures très défavorables**

- — Les exploitations petites : 16 ha en moyenne;
- — Un morcellement important : la moyenne des parcelles est de 30 ares.

### Une agriculture restée traditionnelle

En général les exploitations ont réalisé peu d'investissements importants. Les rendements sont médiocres (2500 l de lait par vache et par an).

### Une agriculture en difficulté...

Tous ces facteurs expliquent que l'agriculture en Livradois-Forez ait connu ces dernières années une certaine régression.

Entre 1970 et 1980, 26% des exploitations ont disparu soit **5 exploitations par commune et par an**, et avec elles, la vie dans de nombreux villages.

Le vieillissement de la population agricole risque d'accentuer ce phénomène : 27% des exploitants ont plus de 60 ans, alors que seulement 9% ont moins de 35 ans (soit 3 fois moins).

Parmi ces agriculteurs qui prendront leur retraite dans les années qui viennent, beaucoup n'auront pas de successeurs.

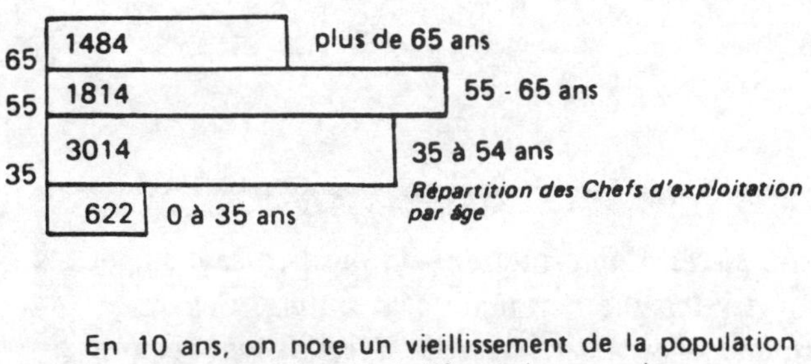


*Répartition des Chefs d'exploitation par âge*

En 10 ans, on note un vieillissement de la population agricole, mais un abaissement de l'âge de la succession.

Le célibat des agriculteurs est inquiétant : 18% des chefs d'exploitation sont célibataires.

La disparition des exploitations ne se fait malheureusement pas au profit exclusif de l'agrandissement des exploitations restantes. Si de 1970 à 1980, la Surface Agricole Utile (S.A.U.) moyenne par exploitation est passée de 13,6 à 16,2ha, soit un accroissement de 18%, il n'y a pas moins de 16 000 ha, soit 12,70% de la S.A.U. qui ont été perdus pour l'agriculture.

Malgré une forte demande de la part des jeunes agriculteurs qui cherchent à s'installer ou agrandir leurs exploitations, ces terres ont été abandonnées à des boisements parfois anarchiques, ou même à la friche, malgré l'existence d'une règlementation. La concurrence de la forêt et la spéculation entraînent un phénomène de **rétention du foncier** qui risque de conduire à la désertification.

### ...mais aussi une agriculture en mutation

Cette régression, que chacun connaît et souligne, ne doit pas cacher une profonde mutation que les agriculteurs du Livradois-Forez ont su mener à bien et qui témoigne de leur dynamisme.

En l'espace d'une dizaine d'années, on a su passer d'une production de veaux de lait, condamnée par le développement des élevages hors-sol, à une production laitière associée à la vente des veaux croisés d'un mois. Cette mutation s'est accompagnée d'investissements importants, en amélioration génétique du cheptel, en matériel et en intensification fourragère.

Ces agriculteurs du Livradois-Forez ont en effet su profiter, pour effectuer une reconversion vers la production laitière, d'une conjoncture favorable où ces veaux croisés de trois semaines destinés à l'Italie, se vendent pratiquement au prix d'un veau engraissé.

Les résultats de l'agriculture du Livradois-Forez doivent être interprétés en relation avec cette mutation.

Les rendements laitiers sont encore insuffisants, mais encourageants, cependant, pour le cheptel en reconversion, si l'on tient compte du lait consommé par les veaux vendus plus tard que dans les systèmes purement laitiers.

Ainsi l'agriculture du Livradois-Forez fait preuve de sa capacité :

— d'élever rapidement son niveau de capital et de productivité,

— de s'adapter avec souplesse à l'évolution des conditions du marché.

### La pluri-activité : une réalité en Livradois-Forez

*La pluri-activité est traditionnelle en Livradois-Forez. Les paysans de cette région ont de tous temps cherché à compléter leurs revenus par des travaux à l'extérieur (coutellerie, papeterie, sciage de long, travail en forêt...).*

*Aujourd'hui, un agriculteur à titre principal sur cinq a une autre activité : activité industrielle (autour de Thiers, Vertolaye,...) ou forestière (Haut-Livradois, Pays de La Chaise-Dieu).*

**Remplissez les cases ci-dessous avec tous les détails nécessaires concernant l'agriculture dans ce parc naturel régional.**

| | |
|---|---|
| Proportion d'actifs agriculteurs parmi les habitants | |
| Principales activités agricoles | |
| Principaux problèmes pour l'agriculture | |
| Preuves de la régression de l'agriculture | |
| Proportion d'agriculteurs de plus de 60 ans | |
| Proportion d'agriculteurs de moins de 35 ans | |
| Proportion d'agriculteurs-chefs non-mariés | |
| Superficie moyenne par exploitation en 1970 | |
| Superficie moyenne par exploitation en 1980 | |
| Superficie perdue pour l'agriculture entre 1970-1980 | |
| Mutation qui a eu lieu | |
| Autres activités entreprises par les paysans pour compléter leurs revenus | |

***Exercise 11** (grid completion) focuses mostly on precise pieces of information - in most cases a single figure or number for each box - and therefore helps to develop the technique of scanning. Generally, more information is sought in such exercises than here and, if well set, exercises like this will require students to collect items of information from different parts of the text. It is sometimes easy for students merely to 'lift' sections of the text without making any effort to understand what they are writing. This can be avoided by asking them to re-phrase their responses, though that obviously makes it more testing. More difficult variations might entail a degree of judgment by the reader ('Exemples d'opinions personnelles', 'Exemples d'exaggération', 'Phrases humoristiques').*

## Exercice 12

**Trouvez dans la liste à droite la phrase qui termine correctement celle commencée à gauche.**

| 1 | 2 | 3 | 4 | 5 | 6 | 7 |
|---|---|---|---|---|---|---|
| | | | | | | |

1 Une foule de visiteurs ____

2 La chaîne des Puys ____

3 La zone des Dômes ____

4 La population des communes à l'Ouest a ____

5 L'installation dans certains secteurs d'une population urbanisée a ____

6 L'agriculture a ____

7 Depuis quelques années, on a quand même ____

A ____ diminué, à cause de l'exode rural.

B ____ y vient profiter de l'environnement extraordinaire.

C ____ entrepris de différentes initiatives pour renouveler l'agriculture.

D ____ possède d'importants restes historiques et archéologiques.

E ____ suscité de nombreux problèmes d'ordre administratif et social.

F ____ subi des changements énormes.

G ____ est une région où l'on peut pratiquer maintes activités de loisirs.

***Exercise 12** (which relates to a text on the effects of tourism in the Auvergne) pinpoints specific sentences or elements of the text for comprehension, but is here made slightly more difficult because the grammatical contexts are similar (all the options begin with a verb, albeit in different tenses). In writing exercises like this, it is essential that all the beginnings of the sentences contain clear signposts relating to the part of the text where the answer may be found, and that they occur in the same order as the text. In this respect, question 1 'une foule de visiteurs' (paraphrase for 'des dizaines de milliers de citadins' or 'visiteurs et touristes se pressent par centaines de milliers') may not be clear enough. This is a vital consideration because the second halves of the sentences are all very much paraphrased; it is tricky enough for students to match the second halves correctly, without having to struggle to identify where the information can be found. An obvious variation is to give students the beginning of the sentence and ask them to complete it. Care needs to be taken to ensure that some manipulation takes place without making it too difficult.*

## Exercice 13

Où est la vérité ? De 1972 à 1982, crimes et délits augmentaient annuellement de 10,25 % en moyenne, alors que la progression n'a été que de 4,40 % en 1983, puis de 3,30 % en 1984 (3 681 453 délits). En fait, quelques optimistes politiques présentent comme une diminution de la délinquance ce qui n'est en réalité qu'une diminution de l'augmentation. Seuls 15 % à 20 % des cambriolages sont suivis d'une arrestation. Est-ce être un obsédé irrationnel de l'insécurité que de percevoir que si « l'augmentation diminue »... cela monte quand même ? De même, les statistiques récemment publiées sur les chiffres comparés du premier semestre 1984 et du premier semestre 1985 sont-elles trompeuses : la délinquance, nous dit-on, a décru de 4,77 %. Le commencement de la fin ? Ce serait trop beau. D'abord, les chiffres pour les six premiers mois de 1985 sont eux-mêmes à peine inférieurs à ceux que l'on enregistrait pour les douze mois de l'année 1973. Où l'on parlait déjà, à l'époque, du « temps des voyous ». Ce qui indique, en gros, qu'en un peu plus de vingt ans la délinquance aurait à peu près doublé. Ensuite, s'il est vrai qu'au total la petite délinquance *répertoriée* a chuté d'une année sur l'autre, il n'en est pas de même pour la grande criminalité, qui, elle, augmente.

Enfin, et surtout, les chiffres ne représentent que les faits constatés, flagrants délits ou enquêtes ouvertes sur plainte. Ils constituent la délinquance officielle.

Il y a loin, on le voit, de la peinture officielle à la réalité. Comme aux Etats-Unis, où l'on se penche depuis lor_ temps sur le « chiffre noir » de la délinquance. Selon une étude du ministère de la Justice américain, le nombre des crimes et délits y dépasse de loin celui qu'indiquent les statistiques de la police. Les vrais chiffres paraissent trois fois supérieurs. Plus de 50 % des viols, agressions, vols qualifiés ne sont même pas signalés. Conscientes du climat détestable que de telles négligences peuvent créer dans le pays, les autorités vont bientôt lancer à la télévision une campagne incitant les citoyens à dénoncer les crimes et les délits dont ils sont les victimes ou les témoins.

**ROGER RAYOT RECORDMAN DES CAMBRIOLÉS**
*112 fois en dix-neuf ans*

**Translate into English the last section of the text from '*Il y a loin*' to the end.**

***Exercise 13*** *reminds us that translation is not entirely dead in the new syllabuses. Usually, students are required to translate only very brief sections, or perhaps to summarise them in English. All modern language teachers are aware that, although students look upon it as an 'easy' exercise, it is amongst the most difficult, demanding complete detailed comprehension and syntactical awareness, along with a good sense of their own language.*

*Inferring meaning/ understanding implications*

Although the number of exercise types in this section is considerably fewer than in the preceding ones, there is a clear distinction to be made between the purpose of the exercises which follow and those which have gone before. The skills demanded are neither purely comprehension nor are they 'free response'; they do not demand simply an understanding of what is in the text, nor do they ask students to stand on their own feet and undertake discussion or carry out a writing task loosely based on the text. Such exercises will naturally be grouped under *Developing writing* (or speaking).

Here, in all cases, students are asked to make judgments, based directly on the context of the text (and therefore, of course, requiring comprehension of a more subtle kind) and to give opinions about character/ideas and, in some cases, evaluate the author's intentions. Generally, exercises falling into this category are likely to be ones associated with literary texts - indeed, teachers keen on the retention of literary study argue that it is this type of interpretative work *inter alia*, which heightens students' awareness on both a human and linguistic level. Literature is a much richer quarry for this kind of work than socio-economic journalism.

## Exercice 14

*Le Tartuffe, Acte II, Scène 4*

**Voici une liste d'adjectifs qui décrivent l'humeur (bonne ou mauvaise!).**

affectueux, amusé, craintif, désespéré, détaché, étonné, fâché, heureux, ironique, joyeux, mollissant, peureux, sarcastique, soulagé, timide, triste, têtu.

**Choisissez dans cette liste celui ou ceux qui sont convenables dans chacun des cas suivants (ou bien ajoutez un mot qui n'est pas dans la liste), pour décrire l'état d'esprit de:**

(a) Valère: lignes 685-6 ____________________

ligne 697 ____________________

ligne 743 ____________________

lignes 752-753 ____________________

(b) Mariane: ligne 694 ____________________

ligne 742 ____________________

ligne 791 ____________________

(c) Dorine: ligne 704 ____________________

lignes 753-757 ____________________

ligne 820 ____________________

**Maintenant comparez votre liste avec le reste de la classe. Si les listes sont différentes, expliquez les raisons de votre choix, et essayez de trouver une liste qui représente une vue commune sur la motivation des personnages.**

***Exercise 14*** *deals with analysis of character. It is relatively straightforward, in that it merely pinpoints a precise location in the text and gives a selection of words from which readers can choose: some of the work is already done for them. However, it could prove quite tricky as a reading exercise and would undoubtedly be easier in response to a performance where the actor's interpretation would be clearer.*

## Exercice 15

*L'Etranger, Deuxième partie, Chapitre 3*
*Travail écrit et oral, à deux*

**Au cours de ce chapitre, dans lequel Meursault se trouve enfin devant la Cour d'Assises accusé de meurtre, ses réactions à ce qu'il voit et entend nous transmettent une impression très claire de son caractère. Avec votre partenaire, considérez les lignes ci-dessous; trouvez le contexte, décrivez-le, puis essayez de décider sur le trait de personnalité que cela révèle. Le premier a déjà été fait pour vous montrer comment.**

| LIGNE(S) | CONTEXTE | TRAIT(S) DE CARACTERE |
|---|---|---|
| Et même, dans un sens, cela m'intéressait de voir un procès. Je n'en avais jamais eu l'occasion. | **un des gendarmes dans la cour lui demande s'il avait le trac** | **manque d'anxiété/ calme/honnêteté/ objectivité** |
| Il m'a fallu un effort pour comprendre que j'étais la cause de toute cette agitation. | | |
| Je me suis expliqué aussi la bizarre impression que j'avais d'être trop, un peu comme un intrus. | | |
| ... malgré mon agacement j'ai pensé qu'au fond c'était assez naturel parce qu'il serait trop grave de juger un homme pour un autre. | | |
| ... pour la première fois depuis bien des années, j'ai eu une envie stupide de pleurer ... | | |

**A la fin, mettez vos idées en commun pour voir si vous êtes d'accord. Est-ce qu'il y a des traits qui se sont révélés pour la première fois ici? Lesquels?**

***Exercise 15*** *is also anchored precisely to the text, but does require an appreciation of the context and, when it comes to the analytical part (column 3), leaves the student to make up his/her own mind, without any 'feeders'.*

## Exercice 16

*L'Etranger, Première partie, Chapitre 4*

**En considérant les réactions de Meursault que vous avez identifiées, choisissez dans la liste d'adjectifs suivants 6 qui vous semblent le décrire le mieux. (Vous pouvez en ajouter d'autres, si vous voulez.) Ensuite mettez-les en ordre de priorité (le no 1 contre celui qui vous semble la meilleure description).**

- honnête?
- simple?
- compliqué?
- sympathique?
- peu sympathique?
- amoureux?
- bête?
- timide?
- courageux?
- superficiel?
- triste?
- extraverti?
- solitaire?
- content?
- intelligent?
- ?
- ?

***Exercise 16**, unlike the preceding two, could form a good basis for discussion and one would expect second year 'A' level students to be able to cope with this type of exercise. It has been included here since it relies on a good understanding of the text and one could expect students to support their responses with examples and illustrations, though it could equally feature as an exercise developing writing skills.*

*Acquiring grammatical/ syntactical knowledge*

All the exercises in this section are concerned with reinforcing or extending students' knowledge of the grammar of the language, or with broadening their appreciation of the way language is structured. Since the eventual purpose of such knowledge is to enable them to produce appropriate and accurate language, particularly in its written form, it might be argued that this is the first step in developing writing skills. However, the placing of grammatical and syntactical exercises in this chapter is intentionally to underline the fundamental importance of reading as the basis for most other language skills. It is crucial for students themselves to understand this point, and to be made aware how focused and thorough preparation of their reading texts (of whatever register) is the key to improvement in all areas of language. Reading should not just be equated with comprehension. Although the dividing line between the development of reading skills and that of writing skills is thin, the exercises in this section have been limited to those which either use reading as a means of teaching specific grammar points which occur in their texts or focus students' attention on language in the texts/exercises which will develop their awareness of stylistic and linguistic patterns as a prelude to their own writing.

## Exercice 17

# A la conquête de l'Europe

**Atoût maitre pour l'Auvergne, le tourisme équestre est bien parti. Et le marché européen semble à portée de sabots.**

"Nous voulons que le tourisme équestre devienne l'un des phares de l'Auvergne ; que partout, l'on rêve de venir chevaucher notre contrée ; que, dans toute l'Europe, l'image de marque de la région soit largement associée à celle du cheval..."

Yves Gratacap ne rêve pas, lui... Depuis plusieurs années, il poursuit cette ambition, et en pose consciencieusement les jalons. Président de l'Association régionale de tourisme équestre (l'ARTE), il agit de concert avec les professionnels membres des associations départementales de l'Allier, du Puy-de-Dôme, de la Haute-Loire et du Cantal.

Et, depuis quelques temps, l'idée se met à galoper... Grâce, en bonne partie, à la "traversée blanche" et au "drag" de la Châtaigneraie cantalienne. Ces deux opérations médiatiques de grande envergure ont frappé les imaginations, attiré l'attention d'une clientèle potentielle et l'intérêt des pouvoirs publics. L'Etat et la Région ont d'ailleurs misé chacun 35 000 F sur la Traversée blanche !

Rappelons-nous... Le 10 janvier dernier, une quinzaine de cavaliers quittaient la station de Super-Lioran pour sept jours de randonnée à travers les monts du Cantal, les Dores et les Dômes pour *"montrer que l'aventure existe là, à deux pas des grandes métropoles, en Auvergne, lorsque la neige a recouvert pour plusieurs mois la route des volcans..."*

Soigneusement organisée, l'expédition rassemble personnalités et journalistes de la presse régionale, nationale et spécialisée, accompagnés de professionnels du cheval. *"Nous avons choisi la traversée du Parc des Volcans parce que celui-ci bénéficie déjà à l'extérieur de la région d'une bonne image de marque*, précise Yves Gratacap. *Nous voulons aussi montrer une Auvergne vivante à travers ses domaines skiables, ses activités agricoles, artisanales, industrielles, touristiques et culturelles".*

L'opération est suivie comme un véritable Paris-Dakar. Les cavaliers empruntent les sentiers délaissés en hiver par les randonneurs et découvrent, émerveillés, les lacs et les vallées glaciaires, les forêts de sapin et de hêtre, la neige et le soleil jouant sur les volcans. Chaque étape bénéficie d'une animation organisée par le Parc et permet d'apprécier l'accueil des élus locaux, conscients de l'attrait touristique de l'opération. A l'arrivée au château de Montlosier, une manifestation réunit professionnels du Tourisme, du cheval et responsables du Parc.

Les médias sont unanimes : *"le tourisme équestre est un atout pour l'Auvergne"*, de même que, *"l'Auvergne, est un atout pour le tourisme équestre"*. La promotion du cheval d'équitation prend un élan extraordinaire : un véritable produit touristique auvergnat vient d'être lancé.

La Traversée Blanche

Pas question pourtant d'en rester là ! L'ARTE a proposé dès le mois de mars, une deuxième opération médiatique : un "drag" touristique dans la Châtaigneraie cantalienne. Autrement dit, une chasse à courre sans harcèlement ni mise à mort du gibier, mais avec tout le faste et l'effort sportif.

Etape suivante : mettre au point ces deux produits afin de les commercialiser dès l'an prochain. Ainsi la Traversée blanche suivra un nouveau parcours et sera proposée à des différentes dates pour planifier l'accueil et éviter une surcharge des hôtels. Et les professionnels se relaieront pour assurer l'encadrement de la chevauchée. L'équipage nécessaire au "drag" se prépare également à "tourner" sur toute l'Auvergne. *"La Traversée blanche et le drag doivent devenir les locomotives du tourisme équestre en Auvergne*, affirme le président de l'ARTE. *C'est à travers des produits haut de gamme qu'il faut lancer une image de marque régionale".*

D'autres activités viennent aussi conforter cette volonté : randonnées à thème dans le Massif Cantalien et le Haut Allier, séjours avec hébergement dans le centre équestre, initiation à la randonnée à cheval, séjours multi-activités dans lesquels l'équitation n'est qu'une partie d'un programme varié offrant planche à voile, canoë-kayak etc...

Les propositions abondent et l'ARTE multiplie les démarches pour que l'Auvergne du tourisme équestre soit présente dans tous les salons du tourisme et du cheval en France et à l'étranger. *"Nous devons penser à 1992.*

*Il faut pénétrer les marchés dès maintenant et mettre sur pied la commercialisation avant l'ouverture des frontières. Sans cela, les Hollandais, les Suédois, les Belges... prendront notre place".*

Grâce à une étude de marché entreprise par la SOMIVAL en 1987, l'ARTE peut affiner ses produits et déterminer les nouvelles orientations. Le tourisme équestre auvergnat prend le mors aux dents et le président de l'ARTE donne de l'éperon : *"Nous ne sommes que soixante-dix-huit établissements professionnels sur la région. C'est trop peu. Plus nous serons nombreux à proposer des produits de qualité et à en faire la promotion, plus le tourisme équestre se développera et plus la région toute entière en bénéficiera".*

Ainsi, le cheval pourrait-il bien devenir la plus noble conquête de l'Auvergne.

**Complétez les phrases suivantes, en utilisant un adjectif de la même famille que le substantif écrit entre parenthèses à la fin. Essayez de faire cet exercice sans regarder le texte, et attention aux accords!**

p.ex. L'ARTE vise à conquérir le marché ______________ (L'EUROPE)
L'ARTE vise à conquérir le marché **européen.**

(a) Le but principal de l'ARTE est actuellement de promouvoir le tourisme ____________________ (L'EQUITATION)

(b) Pour atteindre ce but, le Président coopère avec des représentants des organismes ____________________ (LE DEPARTEMENT)

(c) L'Association ______________ du Cheval participera au travail (LE CANTAL)

(d) Deux opérations ________ont été réalisées pour donner de l'éperon à ce mouvement (LES MEDIAS)

(e) On a fait visiter aux journalistes quelques-uns des domaines ____________ (LE SKI)

## Exercice 18

**Remplissez les cases suivantes avec la forme correcte de ces adjectifs qui se trouvent dans le texte, comme dans l'exemple.**

| MASC (sing) | FEM (sing) | MASC (pl) | FEM (pl) |
|---|---|---|---|
| **bon** | **bonne** | **bons** | **bonnes** |
| européen | | | |
| | régionale | | |
| | potentielle | | |
| | | publics | |
| | blanche | | |
| dernier | | | |
| | spécialisée | | |
| | vivante | | |
| | | | agricoles |
| | | | artisanales |
| | | | industrielles |
| | | | culturelles |

***Exercises 17 and 18**, like a number of grammatical exercises to follow, can be used either as a test (without the text) or as a way of introducing the point. In this case, **Exercise 17** could be given to students with the text. More complex forms of adjectival agreement could be taught, then **Exercise 18** could be set as a follow-up. All the exercises in this section demonstrate ways of teaching grammar in context, mostly without recourse to English.*

## Exercice 19

*L'Etranger, Deuxième partie, Chapitre 4*

**Lisez le chapitre entier. Puis, SANS REGARDER LE TEXTE, complétez les mots dans la section suivante:**

'Moi, j'écout ______ et j'attendais qu'on me jug__________ intelligent. Mais je ne compr__________pas bien comment les qual_________ d'un homme ord_______ pour_____ deven_________ des charges écras________ contre un coup_______. Du moins, c'était cela q________ me frap__________ et je n'ai plus éc___________ le procu ______________ jusqu'au moment où je l'ai enten ___________dire: 'A-t-il seulement exprimé des re_______? Jam ______, mess ______. Pas une seu_______ fois au cours de l'instr____ cet homme n'a paru ému de son abom________ forfait.' A ce moment, il s'est tourné vers moi et m'a désigné du doi________________en contin_________ à m'accabler sans qu'en réalité je comp_______bien pourquoi. Sans d_________, je ne pouvais pas m'empê______ de reco__________ qu'il avait raison. Je ne regr _______ pas beaucoup mon acte.'

***Exercise 19**, depending on the selection of words, can be used either as a comprehension exercise or as a test of vocabulary or grammar. Here, the items are of varying kinds. The exercise is a close relative of the cloze test (see **Exercise 10**). Cloze tests are a popular way of concentrating on given grammatical items (e.g. certain uses of the article, prepositions, passives, etc) and, as with the partially missing words in **Exercise 19**, can be used either to remind or to introduce a new point. In the later stages of the course, one way of consolidating grammatical knowledge is to give students a list of items to be found in the text ('deux exemples de substantifs abstraits', 'un verbe suivi d'un infinitif', 'un participe présent', etc).*

## Exercice 20

**Pour améliorer votre style écrit, l'un des éléments à noter est la structure des phrases. Il faut surtout essayer de varier le début pour qu'il ne commence pas toujours avec le sujet du verbe. Ce texte est particulièrement riche dans ce domaine. Faites une liste de *tous les débuts qui ne commencent pas avec le sujet* (un substantif ou un pronom). Vous n'avez pas besoin d'écrire la phrase entière, mais allez jusqu'au sujet du verbe. La première est déjà faite pour vous montrer comment.**

1 A quelques kilomètres seulement de Clermont-Ferrand, la chaîne des Puys ...

2

3

***Exercise 20** shows how students can be helped to develop a more sophisticated style, and is an exercise which should be introduced at an early stage in the 'A' level course to encourage students away from the simple sentence patterns which many of them will automatically use. They can only do this exercise once they have a reasonable understanding of basic sentence structure, subordinate clauses and so on. The 'collecting' of such patterns, however, should continue and be repeated throughout their course, since without repetition students will revert very easily to using strings of 'standard' sentences. As they become more aware, they can be taught to categorise these openings (e.g. 'expressions qui indiquent le temps').*

## Exercice 21

*Travail écrit et oral à deux*

**Avec votre partenaire, faites une liste pour résumer les problèmes/aspects négatifs auxquels la région des Dômes doit faire face aujourd'hui, selon le texte. Pour chacun, écrivez aussi les mots précis qui servent à créer l'impression négative. Un exemple a été fait pour vous montrer comment.**

| PROBLEMES/ASPECTS NEGATIFS | LANGAGE UTILISE |
|---|---|
| On n'a pas suffisamment exploité le patrimoine historique | 'malheureusement souvent méconnus ou insuffisamment mis en valeur' |

***Exercise 21*** *is a standard exercise for identifying the language used by an author to convey the message. It relates to a text on the redevelopment of the Dômes region. Here, the emphasis is on phraseology. The exercise requires a degree of sophistication, in terms both of comprehension and of language use, in that students are asked in the first column to extrapolate problems from the text and phrase them in their own terms. 'Collecting' exercises can be used on a much broader front, to make on-going lists of functional examples from texts, e.g. 'comment introduire un sujet au début d'un paragraphe', 'comment présenter un argument d'une façon convaincante', 'comment citer l'opinion des autres', 'comment tirer des conclusions'. The intention is to build up a range of language which can be used in both discursive and non-discursive writing. Students should add to the lists continually and monitoring of such work is advised.*

## Exercice 22

# Cocktail Molotov contre restaurant arabe : Deux militaires écroués

A

Deux témoins ont pu communiquer le numéro d'immatriculation de leur voiture à la police. Par chance, le feu n'a provoqué que peu de dégâts. En effet, à cette heure, les deux filles du propriétaire se désaltéraient dans une arrière-salle du restaurant et ont rapidement pu donner l'alerte. Leur père, à l'aide d'un extincteur, a pu limiter les dégâts : trois tables brûlées.

B

MULHOUSE. — Le racisme, que l'on côtoie sous diverses formes dans la vie quotidienne, s'est exprimé de sa manière la plus lâche dans la cité du Bollwerk : lundi matin vers 1 heure, deux jeunes militaires de carrière du 12e RC de Mülheim (RFA) ont lancé un cocktail Molotov dans la vitrine d'un restaurant arabe situé dans la vieille ville, au coin de la rue de la Synagogue et de la rue des Trois-Rois. Et c'est une chance que le début d'incendie occasionné par l'essence enflammée n'ait eu que peu de conséquences.

C

Comment expliquer un tel acte ? Muréna et Lefay ont déclaré qu'ils « détestaient les Arabes ». L'un d'eux milite d'ailleurs au Parti des Forces Nouvelles, mouvement d'extrême-droite qui ne manque pas une occasion de s'en prendre aux travailleurs immigrés.

D

Peu de temps après cet attentat raciste, les deux auteurs ont été interceptés à leur passage au poste frontière de Chalampé. Il s'agit des brigadiers-chefs Daniel Murena, 23 ans, et Jean-Luc Lefay, 20 ans. D'après ce qu'il ressort de leurs déclarations, les deux hommes ayant passé leur dimanche en Alsace sont venus à Mulhouse en début de soirée. De fil en aiguille, pendant leur conversation, portant surtout sur les travailleurs immigrés, l'idée de l'attentat a germé dans leur esprit. En sortant d'un café, ils se sont rendus dans une station-service où ils ont acquis un litre d'essence et d'huile. Au passage, ils ont demandé un chiffon au pompiste. Dans une friterie, ils ont acheté une bouteille de jus de fruit puis ils se sont mis en quête d'un « objectif ». En tournant dans la vieille ville, ils ont découvert la « Palmeraie », restaurant arabe, tenu par un ressortissant algérien.

E

Dans une impasse voisine, Murena et Lefay on confectionné l'explosif puis ils ont mis leur projet à exécution.

F

Pour couronner le tout, par pure bravade, Muréna et Lefay, en quittant Mulhouse, se sont arrêtés dans un café nord-africain pour y boire un verre... Mais ils n'ont pas savouré bien longtemps leur « victoire ». Aujourd'hui, ils se retrouvent en prison. Inculpés par le juge Bietiger de destruction d'édifice habité par explosif — ce qui leur vaudra en principe de passer devant la cour d'assises — ils ont été écroués.

**Les paragraphes de ce texte ont été mélangés. A vous d'utiliser des indications dans le texte pour les remettre dans le bon ordre.**

ORDRE ______________________________

***Exercise 22** requires the re-constituting of a text, the elements of which have been re-arranged in the wrong order. As the text is fairly short, containing six sections, the number of decisions to be made is limited. Although this kind of exercise is generally used to encourage careful reading for **comprehension** purposes, it has equal value in helping students to focus on link words and phrases and on the structure of a text. Great care has to be taken in selecting appropriate texts for such exercises.*

## Exercice 23

**Ci-dessous vous trouverez un commentaire sur chacun de huit tableaux que votre professeur vous montrera, mais les commentaires ont été mélangés et divisés en trois. Mariez les 3 parties (A, B et C) et écrivez le commentaire entier sous le tableau auquel il correspond.**

| TABLEAU | 1 | 2 | 3 | 4 | 5 | 6 | 7 | 8 |
|---|---|---|---|---|---|---|---|---|
| LISTE 1 | | | | | | | | |
| LISTE 2 | | | | | | | | |
| LISTE 3 | | | | | | | | |

LISTE 1

A On voit des personnages de milieux divers qui se côtoient sans se connaître, l'ouvrier en blouse, le bourgeois au chapeau haut-de-forme, la dame au chignon relevé, au-dessus desquels surgit ...

B Dans cette composition aux touches fragmentées et aux tons très rompus de bleu, de vert, de gris et de beige, l'artiste a joué sur l'opposition des lignes sinueuses ...

C Dans cet univers de sable et de mer, tout en gris, ocre et bleu, l'artiste introduit ...

D Dans cette composition de groupe, l'artiste met, pour la première fois, l'accent sur ces musiciens qui passent généralement inaperçus dans un spectacle. La crosse de l'instrument du contrebassiste se détache ...

E Ici, l'artiste s'est attaché à rendre les jeux d'ombre et de lumière obtenus grâce à ...

F Un chef d'oeuvre de jeunesse, ce paysage de neige se veut évidemment réalisé ...

G Deux personnes silencieuses ...

H Un des thèmes favoris de l'artiste à cette époque fut celui des voiliers qui évoluaient sur la Seine. Mais ici les bateaux sont à l'amarre près du pont routier ...

LISTE 2

A ..... sur la scène où, dans l'éblouissement de l'éclairage artificiel, évoluent ...

B ..... l'ombrelle. Le mouvement de la robe et de l'herbe révèle ...

C ..... (la haie et la barrière rustique, la maison paysanne qui évoquent clairement la campagne normande sont précisément décrites) et exclut volontairement toute implication anecdotique. L'objet même de l'oeuvre paraît être la transposition fidèle sur la toile de ...

D ..... et l'artiste a porté toute son attention à la représentation de la surface irisée de l'eau et du paysage qu'elle réflète ...

E ..... devant leurs verres, et qui semblent s'ignorer, ...

F ..... en contrepoint, une petite touche de rouge sur la chaussure de Mme X au premier plan, ...

G ..... de la colline et des arbres aux profils rectilignes des constructions ...

H ..... la serveuse. Tandis que les clients sont tournés vers la scène où se profilent à gauche la robe longue et le bras d'une chanteuse, ...

LISTE 3

A ..... sont assis sur une banquette du café de la Nouvelle Athènes, place Pigalle.

B ..... l'éclat de la neige et de la force des contrastes perçus par l'oeil du peintre sur le motif.

C ..... La facture très précise malgré l'apparente liberté de la touche est tout à fait caractéristique de cette période.

D ..... quelques danseuses en tutus roses et bleus, têtes et pieds coupés, audacieuse évocation du véritable spectacle.

E ..... Le traitement étonnant des parcelles cultivées accentue encore le caractère bizarre de l'espace ainsi figurée.

F ..... la serveuse tourne ses yeux vers un personnage invisible - celui qui regarde le tableau - donnant ainsi la réalité de la vie au tableau.

G ..... qui contribue à créer l'atmosphère lumineuse de cette plage du Nord.

H ..... le souffle du vent; à la marche du personnage répond celle des nuages à l'arrière-plan.

***Exercise 23*** *gives a good idea of how reading can be linked to visual material (such as Impressionist paintings) to extend language. The prime purpose of the exercise is to expose students to language which they themselves might later use for oral or writing purposes. The exercise is clearly quite complex, in that the language is of a literary register and the sentences have to be re-formed, being in three parts. The students may use clues in both the content and the language to tie the various parts of each sentence together. But at the end, they will be more aware of the kind of language which they might use to describe paintings themselves - perhaps in an oral presentation. Another possibility is to provide students with a list of advertising techniques and ask them to match these with a collection of advertisements taken from a French magazine. Visual stimuli provide a welcome change and often generate good responses/discussion beyond the initial exercise.*

## Exercice 24

**écrins**

**DOMINANTE :**
Créé en 1973 parc de haute montagne présentant une très grande amplitude altitudinale (de 800 à 4 102 mètres).
**RAISONS D'ETRE :**
Etendre le parc domanial du Pelvoux créé en 1924 ; protéger ce massif du Haut-Dauphiné situé au cœur d'une zone touristique en pleine expansion ; sauvegarder des systèmes écologiques d'une grande diversité ; améliorer les conditions de l'exploitation pastorale.

**cèvennes**

**DOMINANTE :**
Créé en 1970 ensemble de moyennes montagnes situées au centre même du croissant cévenol, aux paysages d'une exceptionnelle diversité. Parc habité. 550 personnes en 1980.
**RAISONS D'ETRE :**
«Il s'agit non seulement de préserver comme en un sanctuaire des paysages hérités de mille ans d'histoire et qui se dégradent sous les effets de l'abandon, mais aussi d'apporter à ceux des habitants qui s'accrochent encore, des raisons valables de demeurer». A. Monjauze.

**Ecrivez les buts principaux de chaque parc qui sont énumérés dans la section 'Raison d'être'. Attention! Chaque but doit commencer avec un substantif comme dans l'exemple.**

| PARC | BUTS PRINCIPAUX |
|---|---|
| les Cévennes | 1 La préservation des paysages hérités de mille ans d'histoire qui se dégradent sous les effets de l'abandon<br>2 L'apport aux habitants qui s'y accrochent encore des raisons valables de demeurer |
| les Ecrins | 1<br>2<br>3<br>4 |

***Exercise 24** has elements in common with a number of other exercises we have seen. Its purpose it to train students to manipulate language - changing verbs to nouns in specific contexts - and hence to alert them to the fact that different ways may be used to express the same idea. The exercise as reproduced is only part of a longer exercise based on excerpts from five national parks. Other types of manipulation exercise could include transformation of active verbs to the passive, or vice versa.*

## KEY POINTS

- The objectives of the 'A' level course for reading are:

    - to understand and extend vocabulary and idiom
    - to understand general message
    - to understand precise message
    - to infer meaning/understand implications
    - to acquire grammatical and syntactical knowledge

- The acquisition of reading skills is a lengthy and gradual process
- Balance and variety are needed in the selection of reading material
- Texts for use early in the course should be selected carefully
- In-depth study of a few texts is generally better than superficial acquaintance with many
- Proper training in the use of dictionaries is fundamental, particularly monolingual
- The importance of preparation of texts by students cannot be overemphasised
- Students' work on reading exercises needs to be carefully monitored
- The standard threefold approach to setting exercises makes great sense: (1) Working within the text (2) Sorting and practising (3) Working away from the text
- Strategies need to be developed for extending and learning vocabulary
- Linguistic accuracy in reading exercises is always worth fostering, even if inaccuracy is not penalised in some examination papers
- Cloze tests are hard to set - and harder to do!
- Students should not be encouraged to copy sections of a text, but should be encouraged to 'collect' phrases and structures
- Careful, thorough reading can be seen as the basis for the development of all the skills
- Performance in writing hinges closely on good reading habits

## Chapter 3

# DEVELOPING LISTENING

This is the skill which students claim to find most difficult throughout the 'A' level course, despite the increased exposure to authentic listening materials in GCSE. Even so, unlike in reading, their performance at 'A' level is better than they imagine. At the moment, a variety of testing techniques is used by the different boards, but there are signs of a move towards the use of individual cassettes with the facility to listen to material as often as candidates like within a specified time limit. This tends to be popular with students and teachers, since it reduces the stress caused in candidates by the 'single recording for all' situation, in which undue emphasis is placed on memory. It also links closely with good classroom practice. The apprehension concerning the resourcing of this type of activity in schools without language laboratories has been overcome, since the majority of students already possess their own personal stereos and these can be used for homework as well as in class. A note of caution though: it is essential that such machines have a fast-rewind facility.

Clearly, the type of exercise one can set for students will vary according to the playback facility being used. Some of the exercises used in this chapter assume a more traditional format (i.e. a tape recorder being played in class for all to hear - once or twice), but the great majority will be intended for individual playback. This allows students to work at their own rate and provides much more varied opportunities for exploitation.

This chapter will be much shorter than that on reading skills, but this does not mean that less attention should be given to listening. Indeed, the reverse may be true because of its difficulty. However, many of the exercises shown in the first three parts of the reading chapter are equally applicable to listening, and therefore a smaller selection will be shown here. The substantial nature of a reading text (it can be studied more easily, then filed) also makes it appropriate for a wider variety of exercise types.

The majority of 'A' level syllabuses to date have focused almost entirely on non-reciprocal listening, at least as far as their examinations are concerned. However, we should not forget that **reciprocal** listening skills are required specifically in the oral examination and in all forms of oral work we ask our students to carry out, whether 'assessed' or not. Thus, we should build into our course activities which develop this skill, whether they lead to oral or written production. For example, oral presentations by an individual student should never be an excuse for the others in the class to do nothing. They might be asked to react in a number of ways: seek clarification, ask questions, make notes, produce an oral or written summary at the end, conduct a debate centring on issues raised, etc.

Video is currently used only in the Oxford syllabus. But whether its use is developed in future syllabuses or not, there is no doubt that it will form an increasingly valuable part of classroom activities, as the development of satellite TV and/or the direct broadcast of foreign programmes takes place. Although it can be used as an alternative to radio and other recordings for listening practice, its most profitable use appears to be as a stimulus for writing or discussion. Indeed, it is worth mentioning here that listening of any kind can serve as a means of input of ideas and language in the same way as reading, though most of the exercises in this chapter are designed to develop comprehension. As a vehicle for foreign language films, video also enables 'passive' listening. There are many ways in which films can be successfully exploited, but there is some value in giving students the opportunity merely to sit back and enjoy hearing the language for extended periods, as they would if they were in France. Further reference is made to video in Chapter 8.

Transcripts of listening exercises are not included, though they **will** be included in Chapter 6 in the context of a complete mixed-skill unit, where the development of graded exercises within a unit needs to be seen in relation to the recorded 'text' itself.

**Objectives**

Some, but not all, of the skills associated with reading form the bulk of our objectives here:

- ★ understanding and extending vocabulary and idiom (L1)
- ★ understanding general message (L2)
- ★ understanding precise message (L3)

The two which have been omitted are 'Interpreting information/ understanding implications' and 'Acquiring grammatical and syntactical knowledge'. The former is probably too difficult for 'A' level; listening at the level of the first three skills is as much as we can reasonably expect of students, and no syllabus currently requires candidates to go beyond the listening passage itself. The latter (grammar/syntax) is much better taught through the medium of reading texts, and again there is uniformity of opinion amongst boards on this.

**Contexts**

'A' level students should be able to understand the spoken foreign language in the following contexts (though the degree of comprehension will vary, depending on the specific context and degree of difficulty of the material):

- ★ recorded announcements (in public places)
- ★ radio/TV news
- ★ broadcast advertisements (in shops, on radio and TV)
- ★ taped, broadcast or live discussions/interviews on current affairs or topics of general interest
- ★ broadcast documentary material on topics of general interest
- ★ French language films
- ★ contexts which a visitor to France might easily meet
- ★ contexts in which a French speaker might appear in this country
- ★ songs
- ★ a native speaker talking and asking about general interest topics/current affairs
- ★ a native speaker talking and asking about topics prepared by the student

The last two refer specifically to reciprocal listening.

The emphasis given to any 'context' will depend upon the demands of the syllabus, but we owe it to our students to ensure that our courses are not driven solely by the syllabus requirements, so that, for example, whether or not the syllabus makes provision for video or film in its format, the 'A' level student has at the very least a passing acquaintance with the language and culture as expressed in these important expressions of the media.

**Further guidelines**

- **Individual listening**

As much listening as possible should be done via this method - whether in class, using a language laboratory (if available) or for homework (via personal stereos). Where laboratories are too costly, it is worth considering investing in 'junction boxes', which allow several students to listen to a tape at one time.

- **Regular practice**

Little and often is much more effective than very long pieces, which can be very off-putting.

- **Integration within studied topics**
(though current affairs/news may be an exception)

Nearly all the listening we do in real life is 'in context'. We hear an announcement concerning the time of trains at a railway station; we hear news bulletins usually at a time and place when we are expecting them and can link them to what we know about current affairs, etc. It is therefore not only unfair but unrealistic to expect students to listen to the foreign language without some careful contextualisation.

At its very loosest, this will mean simply placing material on acid rain, for instance, within the study of pollution/the environment.

At its tightest it will mean...

**...thorough preparation**

It might be best to consider placing a listening text after reading work, so that some familiarity has already been generated with the language likely to be encountered. In addition, preparation work specific to the listening material will probably need to be done. Different phrases might be given, the main ideas summarised.

- **Clear identification of passages**

One of the major pitfalls to be avoided is that of setting exercises in which students have real problems in identifying the section of the tape which provides the answer(s). At the beginning of every exercise the section should be clearly identified (if there is likely to be any doubt) and short excerpts should be used where possible, so that there are not long passages in the middle of an exercise on which no questions are set.

- **Focused listening**

In most cases, it is important to set clear tasks, not just expose students to broadcast material and allow them to be passive.

- **Graded exercises**

Most language teachers familiar with the new syllabuses take for granted the full exploitation of written texts, beginning with preparation and general comprehension and moving on to more detailed exercises, then finally productive work. The same attention has not really been paid to the listening material. Graded and systematic exploitation is even more important in this area.

- **Proper and complete follow-up work**

Correction of exercises and consolidation of what has been heard are particularly important (with listening exercises in particular there is a tendency to short-change students due to lack of time, difficulty of setting up equipment, etc).

- **Pronunciation and stress**

So often we assume students have the fundamentals when they do not, and much of their difficulty with listening stems simply from their lack of understanding of pronunciation and stress. A very early 'revision' module on this may prove valuable for the great majority of students, since it will aid both listening and speaking skills.

## Developing the skills

*Understanding and extending vocabulary and idiom*

## Exercice 25

Oxford Pack *L'impressionnisme, Première partie, jusqu'à '... qu'il avait peints en 1872'*

**En bas, vous verrez une liste de phrases/expressions qui se trouvent dans l'enregistrement dans l'ordre où vous allez les entendre. A droite, vous trouverez des explications de ces phrases, mais *dans le désordre*. A vous de marier les deux!**

| 1 | 2 | 3 | 4 | 5 | 6 | 7 | 8 | 9 | 10 |
|---|---|---|---|---|---|---|---|---|---|
| | | | | | | | | | |

| Phrases/expressions | Définitions |
|---|---|
| 1 puisqu'il s'agit de | A qu'on connait aujourd'hui |
| 2 d'où vient ce nom? | B contrôlait entièrement |
| 3 que nous connaissons actuellement | C indépendant du Salon |
| 4 pour pouvoir vendre ses toiles | D parce que nous parlons de |
| 5 quels tableaux étaient dignes | E la première s'est déroulée |
| 6 exercent un véritable monopole | F s'il a l'intention de vendre ses tableaux |
| 7 c'était grave | G c'était sérieux |
| 8 hors du contrôle du Salon | H quelle est l'origine du terme? |
| 9 la première a eu lieu | I quelles toiles étaient assez bonnes |
| 10 une toile intitulée | J un tableau qui s'appelait |

*Exercises preparing students for single items of vocabulary are not as useful for listening, since students often have difficulty with the sounds running into each other. It is therefore helpful to explain key/difficult words* **in their context***; this complicates the procedure slightly, since the whole phrase will need definition, but it has the crucial advantage of familiarising the students with the tape they are going to hear. In* **Exercise 25***, some elements are made easy by the inclusion of the same words (salon, c'était). However, the main purpose is to explain and familiarise. Students may often understand the expression merely by seeing it written as opposed to heard, and the definition can be superfluous. This exercise is clearly best done before the tape is heard, by way of preparation.*

## Exercice 26

Oxford Pack *L'impressionnisme, Première partie, jusqu'à '... un des peintres les plus célèbres de l'époque'* (see p 144)

**Utilisez le dictionnaire pour répondre aux questions suivantes.**

**(a) Comment écrit-on en français:**

| | | | |
|---|---|---|---|
| exhibitions | __________ | independent | __________ |
| galleries | __________ | an insult | __________ |
| a painter | __________ | a scandal | __________ |
| conservative | __________ | a refusal | __________ |
| a success | __________ | an example | __________ |

**(b) Donnez l'équivalent en anglais de:**

un siècle __________

le paysage __________

l'époque __________

un vers __________

**Maintenant écrivez toute la phrase dans laquelle vous entendez ces mots.**
p.ex. au milieu du $19^e$ **siècle**

__________

__________

__________

**(c) Dites si les mots suivants sont masculins ou féminins:**

| | | |
|---|---|---|
| monopole | tradition | groupe |
| eau | sensation | exemple |

*Very early in their first term, students will need to learn how to use a dictionary for listening purposes. Given their difficulties in identifying words, and their general propensity for inaccuracy or approximation at this stage, some early exercises, like* **Exercise 26**, *might focus on individual words: (a) how they differ slightly from English words (sometimes); (b) the meaning of some key words (this can be done even if they only have access to a monolingual dictionary) and how these words are being used (i.e. identifying the context); (c) genders (to show that there may be clues in the text or that they ought to check them up if they are unsure). A popular variation is to ask for synonymous words or phrases to be found. This is particularly difficult as a listening exercise unless the extent of the extract is clearly defined and phrases rather than words are sought.*

## Exercice 27

Oxford Pack *La France et les affaires étrangères, jusqu'à '...hésitent'*

**Remplissez les blancs. Les expressions entre parenthèses sont des équivalents des expressions à donner, pour vous aider.**

Sondage: ____________ % des Français croient en ____________________________________ .

____________ d'entre eux pensent que ______________________________________________ .

Bruxelles: On parlait de ______________________________________________ sans pour

autant ______________________________________________ **[aller trop vite]**. Les

ministres n'ont parlé que de la ________________________________________ . Leur seule

préoccupation est ____________________________________________________________

L'UEM ____________ **[n'avance pas vite]**. Ce dossier allait-il ____________ ou____________?

Les Allemands ont voulu ____________________ . Il faut que la RDA poursuive ses réformes avant de

parler __________ ou __________ . Les conditions, ___________ , ___________ et ___________.

'L'Europe reste notre ____________________ . ____________ ne se fera que ____________________

d'une Europe unie.' 'Il faut être ______________ de ce __________'. Sur l'UEM on ______________

**[va lentement]**. Les __________ sont toujours opposés à ______________ d'une __________

_____ et ____________________ . Les ________________ eux hésitent.

> ***Exercise 27*** *is not a cloze test but a straight transcription exercise, with parts of the recording written and words or phrases missing. In the early stage of an 'A' level course, students frequently have difficulty in identifying the sounds they hear as distinct words, and they therefore need assistance in focusing their listening. Although this resembles dictation, its purpose is rather different: it is to show that students have recognised the words being used, and with practice they will be able to identify how the word is written from its sound, even if they did not know it before. As they become more experienced with the language, they can be asked to identify more difficult sections of the passage.*

*Understanding general message*

## Exercice 28

Oxford Pack *Les parcs nationaux, Deuxième section, jusqu'à '... par réaction à la réglementation'*

**Choisissez parmi les phrases suivantes celle qui résume le mieux le contenu de cette section.**

A Les règles strictes du parc national encouragent les gens à réagir contre quand ils sont à l'extérieur.

B Les parcs régionaux sont meilleurs parce qu'ils n'ont pas de règles.

C La réglementation dans les parcs nationaux ne sert pas à grand'chose parce que les gens n'y font pas attention.

> ***Exercise 28*** *is virtually identical to* ***Exercise 7****, though in this case a choice of 'titles' for the section of the text has been given. It could be argued that it would be necessary to understand a fair amount of detail in the text in order to be able to do this.*

## Exercice 29

**Mettez les idées suivantes dans l'ordre où vous les entendez.**

A Les effets de l'accident à Three Mile Island

B Les statistiques concernant la production de l'énergie nucléaire

C Le besoin d'énergie électrique

D Les risques d'un accident grave

E L'effet de la crise d'énergie

F La politique du gouvernement français

G Les avantages du nucléaire

| 1 | 2 | 3 | 4 | 5 | 6 | 7 |
|---|---|---|---|---|---|---|
| | | | | | | |

> ***Exercise 29****, in this instance, is about gist, since it does not require students to have understood any particular details. The only problem with 'ordering' exercises of this kind is that one wrong answer can affect the rest.*

## Exercice 30

**Faites un résumé *en anglais* des passages suivants:**

(a) de la déclaration de François Mitterand (jusqu'à '... élections libres et secrètes')

(b) du commentaire de Georges Marchais (jusqu'à '... qui lui est propre')

(c) de la déclaration de François Mitterand à Strasbourg (jusqu'à '... l'Europe sera l'Europe')

***Exercise 30** is straightforward enough, though much will depend on the amount of detail required. Teachers may vary widely in their expectations, so the important point is to make sure students understand what is being asked of them. Although French is recommended as the medium of communication, to ask students to summarise in French invariably leads to selected 'lifting' of sentences. This can be avoided by insisting on re-wording, but this makes the exercise altogether more demanding - perhaps one which could only be done in the second year.*

## Exercice 31

**Donnez sous forme de titres les grandes questions abordées et les décisions prises au cours de ce sommet:**

1 ______________________________

2 ______________________________

3 ______________________________

***Exercise 31** again focuses on sections of the text, but is more difficult than 29 or 30 in putting the onus on the listener to identify those sections and the appropriate information. In a sense, this exercise bridges the gap between Section 2 'Understanding general message' and Section 3 'Understanding precise message', since the second part of the exercise ('et les décisions prises au cours de ce sommet') is aimed more at detail.*

*Understanding precise message*

## Exercice 32

Oxford Pack *Les parcs nationaux, Deuxième section jusqu'à '... et elle glisse beaucoup moins'*

**Lesquelles des critiques suivantes du parc sont faites par le garde dans cette section? Cochez-les ( ✓ ).**

(a) On ne peut pas mettre des génisses en pâturage dans le parc. ________

(b) Les bergers qui mettent leurs moutons peuvent emmener leurs chiens dans le parc. ________

(c) Le grand public n'a pas le droit d'emmener son chien dans le parc. ________

(d) La réglementation devrait être absolue, sans exceptions. ________

(e) Le parc interdit la construction, mais construit lui-même. ________

(f) Le parc ne fait pas assez pour entretenir les sentiers et les refuges. ________

(g) Le parc permet des survols en hélicoptère pour quelques activités telles l'approvisionnement de certains refuges. ________

(h) Le surpâturage permis par le parc peut causer de graves problèmes. ________

***Exercise 32** is more exacting than a classic vrai/faux, particularly in a listening context, since it will inevitably lead to students replaying the tape on a number of occasions, whilst searching for something which is not there. To avoid too much wasted effort, a time limit should be put on this exercise. As a convention, it is helpful to students always to place the correct answers in the right order, since disentangling them from anywhere on a tape is even more time-consuming and difficult.*

## Exercice 33

Oxford 'A' level listening exam 1990. *Extrait d'une émission consacrée aux problèmes de la pollution dans la société actuelle*

**Complétez les phrases suivantes selon le sens de l'extrait:**

(a) A l'origine la ________ et le ________ étaient les causes de la pollution chimique.

(b) A Pittsburg le soleil brille à peu près ________

(c) Pour la plupart du temps à Pittsburg il y a ________

(d) C'est la pollution ________ qui caractérise la civilisation urbaine.

(e) Les habitants des grands centres urbains ont tendance à souffrir des maladies ________

(f) Celui qui vit dans une grande agglomération a souvent besoin d'un ________

(g) Les sources de la pollution chimique domestique sont ________

(h) ________de personnes ont arrêté de fumer après l'avertissement concernant les rapports entre le tabac et le cancer.

(i) Notre civilisation risque de ________ à cause de la ________ de notre environnement.

***Exercise 33*** *is a paraphrase of the original recording. In most instances, the missing words can be found in the recording, but the sentences printed in the exercise have been re-worded. When setting exercises of this kind it is generally better to be consistent in one's demands on students, i.e. to require only words which appear in the original* ***or*** *words which do not appear but hinge on proper comprehension (in this exercise (f) wants 'psychiatre' and (h) 'peu'; both require a good degree of understanding). However, this exercise has been made a little easier by the use of isolated sentences, focusing only on certain parts of the text, and by using 'signpost words' which appeared in the original, to help locate the answers. In using this kind of exercise to develop listening skills, one needs to move from very easily identified words early in the course to this more subtle form of cloze test in the second year. The ease or difficulty will depend both on the way in which the context is presented (i.e. the words/sentence given) and on the word being sought.*

## Exercice 34

Oxford Pack *Les parcs nationaux, Première section, jusqu'à '... lorsqu'il y a surpâturage'*

**Remplissez les cases ci-dessous avec les détails nécessaires.**

| | |
|---|---|
| Genre de territoire qui peut être classé parc national | |
| Nom du premier parc national du monde et date de création | |
| Date de la création de la Vanoise | |
| Nom de l'animal donnant lieu à la création de ce parc | |
| Effectifs de cet animal en 1963 | |
| Nom du parc voisin italien, et date de création | |
| Effectifs de l'animal aujourd'hui | |
| Situation du parc de la Vanoise | |
| Altitude de la montagne la plus haute | |
| Superficie du parc | |
| Activités encouragées dans le parc | |
| Restrictions au parc mentionnées dans cette section | |

***Exercise 34*** *is clearly the easiest kind of grid, asking students for simple, short facts. It is a good exercise to use if one intends to go on to more difficult tasks based on the same passage, since it gives students a sound grounding in the content at the basic factual level.*

## Exercice 35

*Les informations*

**Normalement, on n'a pas beaucoup de temps pour réfléchir en écoutant les informations de la radio ou de la TV. Après une ou deux écoutes seulement (votre professeur décidera!) vous devez remplir la fiche ci-dessous avec les renseignements essentiels. Ecrivez des notes seulement, pas des phrases entières.**

| REPORTAGE | SUJET | PERSONNES MENTIONNEES | ENDROITS | DATE/ HEURE |
|---|---|---|---|---|
| 1 | | | | |
| 2 | | | | |
| 3 | | | | |
| 4 | | | | |
| 5 | | | | |

***Exercise 35** is included as an example of an all-purpose grid which can be used with any news item (radio or TV). Its great attraction for teachers is of course that it can be brought out at a moment's notice, without any need for preparation. Regular exposure to news should be a feature of any 'A' level course for a multiplicity of obvious reasons, and it is important to give at least some direction to the students' listening. The four elements tend to be covered in most news items, and this format is reasonably straightforward in not requiring further details of the item; they merely have to identify 'le sujet'.*

## Exercice 36

Oxford Pack *L'impressionnisme, Deuxième partie*

**Les expressions à droite sont liées au cours de l'interview aux noms et aux descriptions des peintres à gauche. Pouvez-vous les marier? Il se peut que deux ou trois expressions se réfèrent au même peintre ou au même groupe.**

| A | B | C | D | E | F | G |
|---|---|---|---|---|---|---|
| | | | | | | |

**Peintres**

A les paysagistes académiques
B Corot et les paysagistes de l'Ecole de Barbizon
C Courbet
D Manet
E Baudelaire
F Caillebotte, Mary Cassatt
G Gauguin

**Expressions**

1 le modernisme
2 un paysage imaginaire, idéalisé
3 la réalité sociale contemporaine
4 ne participait pas aux expositions impressionnistes
5 représentait la nature comme lieu de calme et de solitude
6 un des peintres pour lesquels l'impressionnisme représentait un point de départ
7 une lumière artificielle, théâtrale
8 poète de l'époque
9 des idées romantiques sur la nature
10 des impressionnistes moins connus
11 des sujets scandaleux
12 une lumière naturelle

***Exercise 36*** *is similar to* ***Exercise 4*** *(reading), but there are no grammatical clues as to the answers. All the painters are referred to by name, and this provides clear pointers when listening for the answers. In the early stages of a course, the descriptors ('expressions') would either use the exact words of the passage in their entirety, or would be very similar; confidence-building is an important element of developing listening skills. Later on, one can make greater demands by grading the complexity of the re-phrasing so as to make the matching more difficult.*

## Exercice 37

*Travail oral*

**Ecoutez bien la première partie de cet extrait. Ensuite, en utilisant les mots et expressions suivants, commentez *Le Moulin de la Galette* devant la classe et, bien sûr, devant une reproduction du tableau.**

l'effet du soleil - le feuillage - les contours des choses - le sol - les vêtements des couples - taches claires - flotter - exemple important - l'importance de la formation de Renoir de peindre sur porcelaine

***Exercise 37** does not have a direct equivalent among the reading exercises. Although part of its function is to develop oral ability, the effectiveness of the students in carrying out the task will hinge on the extent to which the listening passage was understood. Essentially, it is a summary exercise, but one of a relatively easy kind, since the skeleton of the content is given. The quantity of words/phrases given will dictate the difficulty of the exercise. Although this is only one of two exercises included in the listening skills section which demand an oral response, its inclusion reminds us that we should not think solely in terms of a written response. One of the most obvious comprehension exercise types which has not been included here (Question and Answer in the foreign language) can just as well be done as a communal oral exercise, or in pairs. And although the development of listening skills will mostly take place by giving students the opportunity to listen individually to recorded material, the result of that listening may very well be production of the language in its spoken or written form. (See, for example, exercises 4 and 5 of piece 3 in Chapter 6, 'Producing an integrated unit'; p 136.)*

## Exercice 38

*Travail écrit (basé sur cette partie de l'enregistrement)*

**Expliquez en vos propres termes l'importance pour les impressionnistes:**

(a) des estampes japonaises
(b) de la découverte de la photographie

***Exercise 38** is one of the most difficult of all, since it is the most free. In order to be able to do this, students will need to have understood the original passage, selected appropriate material from it, remembered, then re-phrased it in their own words.*

## Exercice 39

*Découvrir la Savoie (cassette et diapositives)*

(1) L'enregistrement (en 16 sections) a été découpé en 8 parties (8 x 2). Vous et votre partenaire écouterez sections ... . Le professeur vous donnera les deux diapositives qui accompagnent ces sections.

Vous aurez 20 minutes pour écouter, individuellement, les deux sections et pour faire des notes là-dessus (maximum 50 mots). A la fin, le professeur vous demandera de projeter les diapositives et de donner un commentaire sur l'une d'entre elles. Votre partenaire fera l'autre, mais c'est le professeur qui décidera.

Les autres membres de la classe feront des commentaires sur leurs sections, de la même façon.

(2) Pendant les commentaires de vos collègues, il vous faut prendre des notes. Pour vos devoirs, vour écrirez un résumé du programme entier (300 mots)

***Exercise 39**, like **Exercise 37**, is a mixed-skill exercise, linking listening to speaking. As with both Exercise 37 and Exercise 38, it requires skills of summarising a particular section of a recording. Because students know that they have a specific production task to perform at the end, their listening has a more urgent purpose and will invariably be carried out with greater care. If the recording is relatively easy, students should be able to do this early in their course, but care should be taken in selecting appropriate recordings for this exercise. The mixed-skill nature of the exercise can be taken further by completing question 2, which requires further listening (during the commentaries of the other students) plus note-taking, then a final written summary for homework.*

## KEY POINTS

- The objectives of the 'A' level course for listening are:

  - to understand and extend vocabulary and idiom
  - to understand general message
  - to understand precise message

- Most exercises are best done with individual cassettes
- Personal stereos are a useful aid in developing listening skills
- Personal stereos need fast-rewind facility
- Many reading comprehension exercise types can be used for listening
- Reciprocal listening should not be neglected, as listening is not just a passive activity
- Video is an excellent medium for developing some listening skills and as a stimulus for productive skills
- Regular listening - if only to short extracts - is essential
- Lengthy recordings can be counterproductive
- Careful preparation is necessary by the teacher to enable students to cope with listening work
- Exercises should always relate to a closely-defined passage
- It is as important to grade exercises for listening as it is for reading
- Consolidation of listening work is even more important than for reading
- Adequate command of pronunciation and stress is a prerequisite to listening at this level
- Explanation of difficult phrases in advance is important
- Students need to know how dictionaries can help in listening
- Transcription is a useful skill to develop
- Exercises requiring identification of specific words should be avoided - very time-consuming

## Chapter 4

# DEVELOPING SPEAKING

One of the major plusses of GCSE has been the more positive approach students have to oral work, and we should seek to build on this at 'A' level, developing their capacity to perform in more demanding circumstances. It is surprising, however, how limited in scope the vast majority of 'A' level syllabuses are in their approach to testing speaking. Most still insist entirely on a summative test, though the tendency has been to promote internal assessment by students' own teachers, and because of the heavy cost to boards of employing visiting examiners this is likely to become a reality for all oral examining before too long. Hopefully, new syllabuses will appear containing both periodic assessment during the course of normal classes and a much greater variety of contexts than at present - along the lines of the current Cambridge optional scheme.

So it is in the interest of students as practitioners in the language, and in the interest of giving them the best possible preparation for whatever they may be faced by in the examination, that we should seek to develop their oral skills in a wide variety of contexts and for a wide variety of purposes. Ultimately, we are aiming to make students feel as natural as possible in all their contacts with the language. Only by treating communication in the language as 'normal' will they be able to arrive at this goal. Although the recreation of a foreign environment in a particular place (or places) at specific times of the day or week is far short of actually being there, it is important that students are brought as close to this 'reality' as possible. There is no doubt that being in the foreign country for long periods is by far the most effective way of learning the language in all its forms. We can only seek to simulate this and should therefore encourage students to take advantage of all opportunities to speak the language.

The primacy of teaching in the foreign language and of encouraging students to use it as a medium for communication wherever possible means that oral skills are being developed unconsciously all the time and are an ever-present element in a mixed-skill methodology. Virtually any reading or listening exercise can be used to enhance oral performance by adding a phrase such as *comparez votre réponse à celle de votre voisin(e)*, or by setting an exercise as pair work or to be done by general class discussion.

By adopting a *bain de langue* approach, teachers will already be fostering competencies which should take care of a number of the objectives defined below. In fact, all the first section, from 'display the ability to pronounce the language correctly' to 'express a variety of normal emotions and feelings' is likely to be covered by everyday language in the classroom, assuming the normal interchanges likely to take place outside the context of set exercises and activities. Although it is perfectly possible to set specific exercises on pronunciation and accent, the teaching of these aspects of oral work will normally form a continuing part of any 'A' level course and need not be treated separately. Similarly, teachers will no doubt have their own strategies on the question of accuracy.

All the oral exercises in this chapter therefore relate to the second part of the objectives. As with material used for developing other skills, some of the exercises will have a number of purposes or outcomes and should not be looked upon as fulfilling only one function.

Although not all the contexts referred to below are represented specifically in the exercises, material of the kind shown here would prepare students, if used over a two-year period and built on appropriately, to perform adequately in all the situations mentioned.

## Objectives

As with the other skills, we need to establish a clear set of objectives to help us ensure that by the end of the course students can perform appropriately. The syllabuses help us set these objectives in two ways: they define the tasks which candidates will be required to carry out and they publish the criteria which will be used to assess performance. Although 'A' level syllabuses may vary in the precise nature of both these elements, it is possible to establish a set of general objectives which would cover most requirements.

- ★ display the ability to pronounce the language correctly and use appropriate intonation (S5)
- ★ achieve reasonable accuracy in expressing oneself (S6)
- ★ achieve a degree of fluency and responsiveness (S7)

- ★ exchange and communicate information (S1)
- ★ summarise written or heard texts of mother tongue or foreign language origin (S2)
- ★ express and develop ideas and opinions on prepared subjects and subjects of general interest (S3)
- ★ agree/disagree/negotiate/persuade/counter arguments/express a variety of emotions and feelings (S4)

## Contexts

By the end of an 'A' level course, students should be able to perform in all or most of the following situations:

★ conduct an unrehearsed conversation on topics of general or everyday interest with a native speaker
★ conduct a more detailed conversation with a native speaker, on more specialised topics, chosen and prepared by the candidate
★ present an *exposé*, with a minimum of notes, on a prepared topic, with or without illustrative material
★ take part in a debate or discussion on topics of general/current interest with other students or native speakers
★ act as an interpreter for native speakers visiting this country in situations likely to occur (e.g. exchange visitors, formal visitors to school/college)
★ act as an interpreter for English visitors to the foreign country, in regular situations
★ use the telephone for communication with native speakers in a variety of regular contexts

## Further guidelines

- **Small-group work**

Aim to give the opportunity for pair/small-group work every session, however short it may be, but avoid stagnation in student development by variety: vary their partners occasionally and vary the type of activity.

- **Thorough preparation**

Students do not usually have much to say about subjects before they have been given some language and ideas as a starting point. So, generally, reading/listening material is needed first. Whatever the task, it is a good idea to support all oral activities with enabling language.

- **Feasible tasks**

Build confidence (the key to oral performance) gradually by moving from tightly-controlled to more open-ended tasks (*'Discutez la question de la chasse'* may just about be all right in the run-up to the examination, but is likely to lead nowhere earlier in the course, unless properly integrated with other work).

- **Tactful correction**

Keep comment on oral performances private (speaking a foreign language can be a very inhibiting experience, and highlighting an individual's shortcomings can and will compound the problem). Correction of mistakes - as at all levels - is probably best done at the end of the activity. Interrupting students to point out an error undermines confidence and impedes fluency. A balance has to be struck between encouraging communication and confidence and the need to improve accuracy and good language use.

- **Recording performance**

Let students keep personal tapes of their own performance; this will enable them to recognise their progress. They might prefer to record their oral work out of earshot of the whole class. Tapes of this kind should only be played to others with the student's permission.

- **Link with writing**

Oral work will often act as a good preparation for writing, though the reverse can also be true.

## Developing the skills

*Exchange and communicate information*

Generally speaking, the ability to exchange and communicate information ought to be more easily acquired than the other objectives of oral performance, since it will inevitably involve less 'thinking on one's feet'; it is less subject to challenge and interference from other speakers. It therefore lends itself more appropriately to work in the first year of the 'A' level course, though of course that is not to say that it should not be consolidated during the second year. The weaker 'A' level students should certainly be able to cope with this skill, whereas they may have more difficulty with negotiating, arguing, etc. Such students may well not get beyond the exchange of information in some of the exercises intended to develop the 'more complex' skills ('Express and develop ideas...', 'agree/disagree', etc). Implicit in the skill we are examining here is the involvement of another person, though the level of exchange is simply factual and informative.

## Exercice 40

*Travail oral de groupe*

**Posez des questions à vos camarades. C'est pour vous aider à les connaître un peu mieux. Posez un maximum de deux questions avant de parler à quelqu'un d'autre.**

| Trouvez quelqu'un qui | Notez leur nom et prénom |
|---|---|
| habite à (nom de ville) | |
| a toujours habité à (nom de ville) | |
| a habité à l'étranger | |
| est récemment venu à (nom de ville) | |
| habite loin de (nom de ville) (où?) | |
| a deux soeurs | |
| a une soeur et un frère | |
| est un fils/une fille unique | |
| connaît assez bien Paris | |
| n'est jamais allé à Paris | |
| connaît très bien la France | |
| n'est jamais allé en France | |
| a passé les vacances en France cette année | |
| aime faire du sport (lequel?) | |
| aime jouer de la musique | |
| s'intéresse à la musique classique | |
| aime lire (quels auteurs?) | |
| aime la télé (quels programmes?) | |
| déteste la télé (pourquoi?) | |

## Exercice 41

*Travail oral à deux*

**Vous connaissez déjà un petit peu vos camarades de classe. Mais savez-vous poser des questions?**

**(a) Décidez avec votre partenaire comment vous poseriez des questions à quelqu'un pour savoir ... (n'écrivez rien!)**

1 leur nom (p.ex. Comment tu t'appelles?)

2 l'endroit où ils habitent

3 s'ils ont des frères ou des soeurs

4 ce qu'ils aiment faire

5 l'endroit où ils ont passé leurs vacances

6 s'ils aiment faire du sport

7 leur âge

8 les raisons pour lesquelles ils ont choisi d'étudier le français

**(b) Changez de partenaire et posez-lui ces questions pour tout savoir sur lui/elle. A la fin, changez de rôle.**

***Exercises 40** and **41** show how very straightforward activities can be devised right at the beginning of the course to help 'break the ice' and enable students to get to know one another (particularly useful in sixth form colleges etc). **Exercise 40** spoonfeeds the students by assuming the same format throughout ('Est-ce que'), with minimal changes to the verbs. The nervous can restrict their responses, but stronger students should be encouraged to develop them (at all times). **Exercise 41** can be done quickly after, requiring preliminary preparation with a partner for part (a), and then the memorising of a variety of question forms for part (b). The exercises help establish the principle of group interaction from the beginning.*

## Exercice 42

*Travail oral préparatoire*

**Peut-être que vous vous intéressez déjà à la peinture ou peut-être que vous ne commencez qu'à la découvrir. Répondez aux questions suivantes, en donnant autant de détails que possible dans vos réponses.**

Voici quelques expressions pour vous aider:

- j'aime beaucoup ________
- j'aime surtout ________
- je n'apprécie pas tellement ________
- je suis très attiré(e) par ________
- l'oeuvre de ________ me passionne
- les tableaux de ________ me touchent beaucoup
- ce qui m'intéresse/m'attire/me captive/me séduit/me fascine chez ________ c'est ________
- j'ai entendu parler de ________
- je connais un peu l'oeuvre de ________

(a) Est-ce que vous aimez regarder les tableaux?

(b) Vous est-il arrivé récemment de visiter une exposition?

(c) Quel genre de peinture préférez-vous?

(d) Préférez-vous les paysages, les portraits, les natures mortes ...?

(e) Faites-vous vous-même de la peinture, ou des dessins?

(f) Combien de peintres français pouvez-vous nommer?

(g) Connaissez-vous déjà quelques peintres impressionnistes?

(h) Pouvez-vous nommer quelques tableaux impressionnistes?

***Exercise 42** is an example of the simplest form of oral interchange - question and answer, designed to elicit information. Normally, quizzing students in this way in front of their colleagues is not the most effective way to encourage them to speak, particularly if the group is a large one, and is therefore best left to be done in pairs, but the intention of this exercise is to act as a general introduction to a new topic with its new vocabulary and concepts. The questions are designed to provoke simple replies, to show that there may be something they know which they can build on, rather than expose their lack of knowledge at the start. Although opinions are asked for, it is at a superficial level. As before, it is helpful to provide them with words and phrases which could be used to frame their replies. The same exercise can be consolidated in pairs.*

## Exercice 43

*Que savez-vous de votre parc national/régional?*

*Première partie - préparations (devoirs):*

**Le professeur distribuera les trois dépliants publicitaires concernant les différents parcs parmi les membres de la classe (si vous en avez obtenu d'autres, tant mieux). Individuellement vous devez étudier de très près 'votre' parc, pour pouvoir répondre à des questions là-dessus en classe. Vous ne pourrez pas utiliser des notes; il faut donc tout mémoriser.**

*Deuxième partie - travail oral:*

**En groupes de 3 personnes (4 ou 5 si vous avez d'autres dépliants), chacun ayant préparé un parc différent. A tour de rôle vous devez répondre aux questions des autres membres de votre groupe qui veulent tout savoir sur votre parc.**

**Voici une liste des aspects qui pourraient être traités, pour donner aux autres membres du groupe des idées pour des questions. (Ne vous limitez pas à ces aspects - essayez de penser à d'autres questions!)**

- situation géographique
- relief
- villes principales
- accès
- richesses naturelles: flore et faune
- activités traditionnelles
- équipements touristiques
- patrimoine historique/culturel, etc

***Exercise 43*** *requires rather more confidence and skill, since (in this version) it stipulates no use of notes. During their course, students will need to develop presentational skills (referred to in more detail in the section beginning on p 86, 'Express and develop...'), and to learn how to convey verbally information they have read/researched. This exercise has close links with the summarising of reading passages and the presentation of more extended exposés, but here there is the opportunity for them to express the material as fully as possible and to respond to questions from other students on their material. By doing the same exercise several times within the group, they will learn phrases and techniques from each other. The teacher's role during this kind of activity is problematical: to listen (and presumably comment later), merely to listen, or to 'disappear' and play no part in it? There is something to be said for the latter, though much will depend on the students involved and their degree of confidence.*

## ▼ Exercice 44

*L'Etranger, Première partie, Chapitre 6*
*Travail oral à deux*

**La police interroge tous les témoins des événements de la journée: Raymond, la femme de Masson, Marie, Meursault, et un des Arabes.**

**La classe se divise en paires, et les rôles des témoins sont distribués parmi les membres de la classe. L'un d'entre vous jouera le rôle du policier et remplira la fiche ci-dessous, selon les renseignements qu'on vous donne. L'autre jouera le rôle du témoin (p.ex. Raymond).**

**(Pour remplir la fiche, le policier pose des questions comme: 'A quelle heure, précisément? Avec qui? Pourquoi? Qu'est-ce que vous avez vu? Que faisait X à ce moment-là? etc)**

| CONSTATATION DE | |
|---|---|
| ADDRESSE | |
| DATEE LE | |
| | |

***Exercise 44** shows how a more imaginative format can sometimes be devised for role-play exercises. It is more subtle in its requirements than Exercise 43 because there are no guidelines on which to work, there is no consolidation within a group, and much will depend on the extent to which a student has read, understood and remembered a detailed section of L'Etranger. Clearly, much will depend on the quality of the questioning by the student playing the policeman, and care should be taken to select the stronger students for that role.*

*Summarise read or heard texts of mother tongue or foreign language origin*

Some examination boards include this exercise as part of their oral assessment. Realistically, the most 'authentic' exercise of this type would probably be to get students to summarise a French text in English, since that is a more likely situation for them to find themselves in. However, since the main thrust of our teaching now is to develop linguistic competence, it is more appropriate to develop the skill French-to-French. The Oxford syllabus currently requires candidates to summarise an English piece in French, in contexts which could easily occur for foreign language students.

Since this skill is very clearly defined and rather narrow, there are not many different ways in which it can be developed - hence the limited number of exercises. In a sense, one might have included this skill as a sub-section of Section 1 (*Exchange and communicate information*), but there is a significant difference between the two, since 'summarising' does not generally imply any response from the listener - though in the case of examinations, the examiner may well prompt if the candidate dries up. Summarising without interaction is probably more difficult than exchanging information, as it will require a selection of material by the student as well as re-phrasing and a degree of independence.

## Exercice 45

*L'Etranger, Première partie, Chapitre 5*
*Travail oral à deux*

**A tour de rôle, vous reconstituerez la description de ce que Meursault a vu chez Céleste. Vous utiliserez les mots-clés suivants, et vous commencerez par "J'ai dîné chez Céleste ..." (Ne regardez pas le texte!)**

femme - s'asseoir - gestes saccadés - jaquette - carte - plats - sac - l'addition - somme exacte - hors d'oeuvre - crayon bleu - magazine - coché - émissions - remettre sa jaquette - sortir - trottoir - suivre son chemin - bizarre - oublier

***Exercise 45** could be applied to any narrative situation, merely requiring students to reconstitute a small section of the text from key words - albeit transposing from the third to the first person. This skill can be built up by using gapped texts of the original, but gradually expanding the gaps until only a few words remain. When asking students to perform one-sided tasks like this, it is always useful to ensure that the second student in the pair has a function. Here, it is simply to listen, prompt (where necessary) and then fulfil the same role, hopefully more successfully. Thus it makes more sense for the stronger student to go first, so that the weaker of the two can learn. The engineering or manipulation of pairs in this way is neither always possible nor desirable. Most pairs 'self-select', and this is generally best left to the students, since they will work better with someone of their choice. Often, they establish regular partners of similar ability. Nonetheless, it is good for everyone to change round from time to time to avoid staleness. A 'fun' variation could be to get students to reconstruct an entirely different (imaginary) story using the same prompt words.*

## Exercice 46

**Vous devez faire un reportage d'une minute à la radio sur la 'yougo-connection'. En vous servant des faits donnés dans le texte d'écoute et dans cet article, préparez votre reportage. Les titres suivants vous aideront à le structurer:**

1 Définition de la yougo-connection
2 Leur terrain d'action et leurs modes d'opération
3 L'impuissance de la police
4 L'exploitation des enfants
5 Solutions

**Quand vous faites votre reportage vous pouvez utiliser seulement les titres ci-dessus.**

***Un réseau de la « yougo connection » démantelé à Paris***

# *Quatre protecteurs des enfants voleurs arrêtés*

***avec la « recette » d'une journée : 40.000 francs***

LA traite des enfants redouble à Paris en ces mois d'été. La Brigade de répression du banditisme en a la preuve. Elle vient pourtant de frapper un grand coup en démantelant l'un des principaux réseaux affiliés à ce qu'il est convenu d'appeler la « yougo connection ».

**Ainsi est-elle parvenue mardi à interpeller en flagrant délit quatre personnes — trois adultes et un mineur — presque tous membres de la même famille, spécialisés dans la « protection », et l'encadrement des enfants qu'ils ont eux-mêmes dressés à dévaliser les touristes dans les lieux les plus fréquentés de la capitale en ce mois d'août et notamment, bien sûr, aux abords du Louvre qui constitue leur terre d'élection.**

**Les policiers ont réussi à récupérer la recette de la journée des enfants voleurs : 10.000 marks (32.500 F.) et 2.000 francs suisses (8.000 F) !**

Ils étaient depuis plusieurs jours sur la piste de ces malfaiteurs — mais le terme malfaiteur parait bien modeste en regard de l'ignominie des personnes — et il ne leur manquait qu'une occasion de passer à l'attaque à coup sûr.

Ils avaient remarqué que les « protecteurs » de la yougo-connection convoyaient chaque jour à bord de puissantes voitures une noria de petits gitans qu'ils « lâchaient » aux abords du Musée du Louvre et qu'ils venaient rechercher le soir pour empocher le butin. **Ils les ont suivis jusqu'à leur campement puis ils ont bouclé le quartier et ont fouillé partout.**

Dans la voiture de Raif Hamidovic, vingt-deux ans, originaire de Zagreb, ils ont découvert un fusil Riot Gun approvisionné et la recette quotidienne des petits voleurs. Les autres personnes interpellées sont Zarif Hamidovic, vingt-deux ans, Bezo Hrustic, vingt-quatre ans, et un autre membre de la famille Hamidovic, mineur celui-là puisqu'il est âgé de dix-sept ans.

### Six identités

**Si, chaque année, des dizaines, voire des centaines d'enfants voleurs sont arrêtés avant d'être relâchés quelques heures après, il est plus rare que l'on parvienne à identifier les adultes qui en sont les tuteurs ou simplement qui en ont la responsabilité.** Or, on sait que la loi française est démunie dès lors qu'il s'agit de sévir contre des enfants de moins de treize ans pour lesquels la prison est interdite.

Entre treize et quinze ans, la peine ne peut excéder dix jours. C'est l'une des raisons pour lesquelles les petits Yougos du Louvre, parfaitement informés de ces dispositions légales, n'ont jamais sur eux le moindre papier d'identité. Ils prétendent chaque fois être âgés de moins de treize ans, ce qui est d'ailleurs, en effet, souvent le cas. **Il y a deux ans, la B.R.B. a arrêté un de ces mineurs pour la vingt-deuxième fois. Elle le connaissait sous six identités différentes.**

Les grandes tribus gitanes sont installées depuis une dizaine d'années dans des campements à Montreuil ou au bois de Boulogne. Cette fois encore, c'est près du bois de Boulogne, non loin des rives de la Seine, que s'est déroulée l'opération de police.

Ces petits Yougos si prodigieusement habiles, on estime qu'ils sont environ trois cents à Paris, pas davantage. **Chaque équipe — deux ou trois gamins — peut rapporter jusqu'à 30.000 F ou 35.000 F par jour, sans parler des montres ou des bijoux. Ils font l'objet d'un véritable trafic, notamment entre la Yougoslavie et l'Italie. Avec d'inévitables prolongements en France.**

### Prestidigitateurs

**Ils vivent en vase clos, repliés sur eux-mêmes, sans contacts avec le monde extérieur. Ils sont le gagne-pain, le trésor de la tribu. Ils en sont aussi les esclaves... parfois consentants.**

Récemment, les enquêteurs de la brigade de répression du banditisme dirigés par le commissaire Raymond Mertz, se sont rendus en Yougoslavie pour tenter de s'attaquer aux racines du mal. **Ils ont rencontré leurs homologues de l'Est qui leur ont confirmé l'existence d'un trafic d'enfants.**

**Les gosses sont pris en charge par des adultes qui leur apprennent à voler jusqu'à en faire de véritables prestidigitateurs. Jusqu'à téléguider leurs mains et parfois leur esprit. Ils entrent en France avec les adultes grâce à un passeport muni d'un visa de tourisme valable pour trois mois. Et puis, ils ne repartent jamais.**

**Jean-Michel BRIGOULEIX**

## Exercice 47

### THE CHANNEL TUNNEL: RECENT DEVELOPMENTS

A wider perception of potential benefits associated with the Tunnel is developing nationally in both countries.

In the UK a study of the tunnel's potential to generate new tourism business was undertaken during 1987 under the auspices of the British Tourist Authority. In conjunction with British Rail, Eurotunnel also launched a regional study of industrialists' and local authorities' perceptions of commercial and cost saving opportunities which might be associated with Tunnel services.

A major development during 1987 was the announcement of the massive Euro Disneyland leisure complex development east of Paris, due to open in 1992. A TGV link to the complex is under consideration, which would enable it to be reached in just over 3 hours from London.

In the UK the sections required to complete the M20 motorway are at an advanced planning stage, and a second Dartford crossing of the Thames is going through the Parliamentary approval process. In addition, there are a number of improvements planned in Kent to roads which connect to the Tunnel. In France the A26 motorway is being extended towards Calais, and a new expressway is now in the course of design and construction which will connect Eurotunnel's terminal at Coquelles directly to it.

Regarding rail infrastructure, in the UK British Rail is committed to substantial expenditure on improving the line between the Tunnel and the new international terminus to be built at Waterloo.

In October 1987 the French Government announced its decision to permit SNCF to proceed with the construction of a new high speed (some 300 km/h) line between Paris via Lille to the Belgian border, with a connecting spur to the Tunnel.

Agreement has been reached between the three railways, British Rail, SNCF and SNCB (the Belgian national railway) concerning high speed services between Paris and London and Brussels and London.

**SITUATION:** Vous passez deux semaines chez votre correspondant(e) français(e). Vous avez une brochure sur le tunnel sous la Manche en anglais.

**TACHE 1:** Un soir après le dîner vous parlez avec le père/la mère de votre correspondant(e) (l'examinateur), qui ne comprend pas très bien l'anglais. Vous lui expliquez ce qu'il y a dans la brochure sur le tunnel.

Il n'est pas nécessaire de traduire le texte. Essayez plutôt d'en résumer les aspects principaux.

***Exercises 46 and 47*** *are both examples of the target skill; students have to summarise either part (46) or the whole (47) of the text.* ***Exercise 46****, though longer, is marginally easier, since certain indicators are given as to the content and may be used as prompts. Here, a realistic context is given to give added point to the exercise (and radio report).* ***Exercise 47*** *is an actual example of an 'A' level test. Candidates may make notes, but otherwise no prompts are given on paper. The examiner may prompt where the candidate is having difficulty. In preparing for this kind of exercise, students should be encouraged to ensure that the content of each paragraph is covered, but not to translate word for word.*

*Express and develop ideas and opinions on prepared subjects and subjects of general interest*

In the context of 'A' level oral examinations, students have always been required to converse on matters of general interest. For many years the format was a reading passage followed by general discussion. This is now tending to disappear in favour of a more defined discussion, normally on a topic or topics prepared by the student, sometimes preceded by a brief uninterrupted presentation by the student of the topic. The amount of time allowed for the preparation varies; in some cases there are no limits imposed, in others a specific topic or choice of topics may be given to the student at a specified point in the run-up to the examination. The rationale behind the prepared topic discussion which, in most cases, can be led by the student (often he/she is required to provide a list of areas to be covered), is that it affords the student the opportunity to set the agenda and show what he/she can do at best. Before, the hit-and-miss nature of the discussion could seriously disadvantage candidates. Clearly, all the input of work on a given topic (reading, listening, oral and writing) will serve as an important preparation for oral work in which they will be expected to express their ideas. The three types of activity in this section are broadly representative of the kind of exercise commonly in use in the new French courses. Though not specifically linked (the first two relate to impressionism, the third to other topics), they are progressively more demanding, both in technique and content. Attached to the final exercise is a supporting sheet (see p 92 *Ressources de soutien no 1, no 2*). Such additional support is vital in cases where students have a degree of autonomy and where the use of a resource bank is implied.

## Exercice 48

*En commençant à regarder des tableaux (à faire avec un choix d'illustrations/diapositives)*

**Le contenu**

- Quel est le sujet de ce tableau? Décrivez-le.
- A quel aspect de la vie l'artiste s'intéresse-t-il? Comment savez-vous cela?
- Est-ce que ce tableau contient des symboles? Lesquels? Qu'est-ce qu'ils représentent, à votre avis?

**La composition**

- Quels sont les éléments importants de la composition? Lesquels sont dominants? Lesquels sont moins importants?
- Vers où vos yeux sont-ils attirés?

**Les couleurs**

- Quelles couleurs a-t-il utilisées? Sont-elles réalistes? Pourquoi?
- Est-ce que les couleurs sont typiques de l'artiste?
- A-t-il utilisé des couches très épaisses ou voyez-vous des traits de pinceau individuels? A-t-il tracé les contours? Quel est l'effet de cela?

**Conclusion**

- Pourquoi l'artiste a-t-il choisi ce sujet?
- Quelles impressions avez-vous de l'atmosphère créée dans le tableau?
- Quelles techniques l'artiste a-t-il utilisées pour créer l'atmosphère?
- Aimez-vous ce tableau? (Votre professeur vous dira qui a exécuté chaque tableau, et à quelle date.)
- Pouvez-vous comparer ce tableau avec d'autres du même sujet que vous connaissez?

***Exercise 48** is a progression from **Exercise 42**. It is designed to be done with the class as a whole, but this time not limited to the transfer of factual knowledge. The questions are intended to introduce students to the concepts and basic techniques of painting. In this, the teacher will need to play an important part, feeding the students with appropriate language and ideas if necessary. Since looking at pictures is probably something which most students have not done before, the questions should not be looked upon as prescriptive, but as a starting point only. Hopefully, the students themselves will suggest others, and they should be encouraged to be as analytical as possible; to begin with the factual, but to attempt to draw conclusions. The group format, in which the less assertive students will doubtless remain silent, should not be adopted wholesale. This particular activity could easily be done in pairs later (with different paintings).*

## Exercice 49

*Travail oral: le Moulin de la Galette (Renoir)*

(a) **En groupes de 3 ou 4:**

Regardez bien ce tableau et imaginez que la radio a été prématurément inventée. Vous avez dix minutes pour préparer un reportage sur les loisirs dominicaux des Parisiens, comme ils sont représentés dans le tableau.

Qu'est-ce que vous pourriez dire sur cette scène? Les bruits, les activités, les sentiments, l'atmosphère?

(b) **En paires:**

Avec un partenaire qui était dans un autre groupe, préparez finalement ce reportage. Vous avez seulement cinq minutes. A la fin, enregistrez votre reportage, qui doit durer deux minutes, au magnétophone.

(c) **Devoirs:**

Choisissez individuellement une autre scène peinte par un impressionniste et soyez prêt(e) à la décrire devant la classe. Vous pouvez vous référer à toutes les autres activités qu'on a faites sur les tableaux pour préparer le vocabulaire et les phrases nécessaires.

(d) **Travail à deux:**

En classe, après les petits exposés sur les scènes différentes, faites une liste des aspects de la vie représentés par les impressionnistes (p.ex. l'animation dans des restaurants célèbres).

Quelles conclusions pouvez-vous tirer de ce choix? Ensuite, mettez vos idées en commun avec le reste de la classe.

***Exercise 49** is a suite of activities mostly intended for small-group work, embodying a vital principle of oral development; the more one prepares for a particular task, the better it is likely to be performed (within reason). Thus activity (a) puts no pressure on students, enabling them to produce ideas collectively, and (b) permits them to repeat the material just produced, but modifying/expanding it by covering the issue with fresh ideas before making the 'final production'. All the work done so far will inform students' individual work on (c), and they should have no difficulty presenting their own ideas on a chosen painting in class before (d) further follow-up work in pairs. By the time they reach the last part, they should be in a position to draw some sensible conclusions.*

## Exercice 50(a)

*Exposés individuels: la crise de l'énergie*

**(a) En utilisant les textes que vous avez déjà étudiés, ainsi que vos propres idées, préparez un exposé individuel sur l'un des sujets suivants. Vous devez parler devant la moitié de la classe pour 3 minutes. Il ne faut pas écrire ce que vous allez dire, mais vous pouvez utiliser des notes (maximum 25 mots!).**

1 Pourquoi nous devrions développer l'énergie solaire
2 Pourquoi nous devrions développer l'énergie hydraulique
3 Pourquoi nous devrions développer l'énergie éolienne
4 Pourquoi nous devrions développer l'énergie nucléaire
5 Pourquoi nous ne devrions pas développer l'énergie nucléaire
6 Pourquoi nous devrions développer l'énergie géothermique
7 Pourquoi nous devrions économiser l'énergie
8 Comment nous devrions économiser l'énergie

**(b) La classe est divisée en deux. S'il y a plus de 8 membres, il faut que les personnes ayant préparé les mêmes sujets soient dans des groupes différentes. Les étudiants dans chaque groupe font leur exposés (3 minutes chacun).**

**Après chaque exposé, un autre membre du groupe essaie de reproduire autant que possible l'exposé qu'on vient d'entendre. On fait ceci à tour de rôle!**

*The third means of developing this skill puts the individual student at the centre of the work. Individual presentations in French on a topic or an aspect of a topic being studied have much to commend them, and the exercise shows how specific aspects of a topic can be targetted for a brief presentation. Providing the class is large enough it is a good idea to split them into two groups, so that students only have to talk to half the class. This kind of build-up exercise is very useful before asking students to take on a lengthier exposé (as in* ***Exercise 50(b)****). The requirement to get students to give a summary, in turn, of what they have just heard (section (b)) is one means of ensuring that they listen to what is being said! An essential ingredient of this type of exercise is that students do not see it as a writing and reading activity. Various strategies can be adopted to encourage them to use notes: an alternative to limiting the number of words is to insist that the notes are written on an OHP transparency and used in that way.*

## Exercice 50(b)

*Exposé oral devant la classe sur une région de France*

**Vous devez faire un exposé oral devant le reste de la classe sur l'une des régions de France. La distribution sera faite en groupe pour éviter que tout le monde choisisse le même sujet. Votre professeur vous dira combien de temps vous aurez pour préparer le travail et vous indiquera le jour de la présentation.**

L'Auvergne
L'Alsace-Lorraine
L'Aquitaine
La Bretagne
La Bourgogne
Le Languedoc-Roussillon
Le Nord - Pas-de-Calais
La Normandie
La Provence - Côte d'Azur

**l'Ardèche**
**la Dordogne**
**la Seine**
**le Rhône**
**la Loire**
**La Corse**

**Voici les instructions:**

★ Votre exposé doit durer au moins 10 minutes

★ Vous pouvez utiliser seulement une page de notes (à montrer au professeur un jour avant!)

★ Vous devez être prêt(e) à poser des questions à vos collègues au cours de l'exposé, ainsi qu'à répondre à leurs questions

★ Vous devez utiliser des photos/affiches/livres/diapos pour illustrer l'exposé

★ N'oubliez pas de parler de:

- la géographie physique de la région
- son histoire
- ses activités industrielles/agricoles
- l'importance du tourisme et ses attraits
- vos opinions personnelles et des conclusions que vous avez tirées de vos études

***Exercise 50(b)** assumes an in-depth study which will lead to a major production, lasting sometimes between 15 and 30 minutes. The length, format and purposes may vary from time to time, from school to school or class to class. Like coursework, it offers the chance for students to work at their own pace; it offers the opportunity for a variety of different experiences within the course which should lead eventually to more varied essays on the topic (this is quite important for big centres in which there may be a tendency for all students to write the 'same' essay in an examination); it gives added motivation to students who may become stale following the normal routine of work; it allows for a truly mixed-skill approach, and so on. Consequently, such activities look set to be a regular feature of sixth form work in the future.*

*Before embarking on work of this kind, where the students are being called to perform very much on their own, it is vital to prepare them thoroughly first. The following points should be borne in mind:*

- *The very notion of speaking in French in front of the rest of the class (particularly if the class is large) could and does frighten students. It is therefore not something which should be attempted 'out of the blue' or very early in the course.*
- *Gradual confidence-building is necessary first - perhaps by asking students to do shorter activities in front of a third or half the class.*
- *The nature of the task should be made clear (see p 92, Ressources de soutien no 1), though psychologically it is wise to understate the time they will be expected to speak. Ten minutes is generally acceptable.*
- *The assessment procedure for the activity should be explained from the outset, to help students set their objectives and prepare themselves adequately.*
- *They should be provided with a list of resources which they can use (see p 92, Ressources de soutien no 2).*
- *A session pin-pointing some useful techniques they can use is very helpful at the start (e.g. how to structure the talk, techniques for explaining and re-phrasing, techniques for involving the other members of the class, how to use 'visuals'), although a 'model presentation' is probably not a good idea, since it will give them preconceived ideas of exactly how to go about it and will either frighten them (if too good) or limit them in expectations (if pitched too low).*
- *Students should be encouraged to use visual aids: slides, illustrations, OHPs, etc. These will add interest and variety to their talk.*
- *Preparation time should be carefully allocated. Again, this will depend on resources and expectations/objectives. It is helpful to students to be given some class contact time to draw a measure of support from the teacher.*
- *There is a real danger of student boredom after the first two or three presentations, when larger classes are involved. Several strategies can be adopted: put a time limit on the students if they begin to get lengthy; do not give all the class presentations to do at the same time - rotate them throughout the year; interpose presentations with 'regular' classes (this will spread them over a longer period, but may be much more acceptable); pair up students for presentations - this reduces the length by nearly a half and gives them mutual support, a good strategy when doing presentations for the first time. Additionally, one can insist on the involvement of other students, by allocating a substantial proportion of the total marks to the student's participation in everyone else's presentations. This mark (say 25-30%) can be judged by quality as well as quantity of interventions, though one has to be careful to ensure the quieter/weaker students don't get steam-rollered!*
- *A second danger is that once their own presentation is over, students may have no homework to do for quite a lengthy period. This can be avoided by setting some parallel homework, reading or listening exercises, which has to be done over the same period. Those who have their presentations early in the sequence do their other homework afterwards, the others may have to do it early on.*

*Ressources de soutien no 1: Comment faire un exposé oral*

**Voici un ordre d'activités que vous pourriez suivre pour préparer votre exposé.**

1 Cherchez tous les documents mentionnés dans la liste de ressources que votre professeur vous a donnée.

2 Décidez dans quel ordre vous allez les étudier; est-ce qu'il y en a qui paraissent plus importantes que d'autres?

3 Faites des notes sur ce que vous lisez/écoutez; mais gardez ces notes d'une manière organisée (par exemple, une page pour 'l'histoire' etc). Ecrivez en même temps des phrases/expressions/vocabulaire utiles.

4 Décidez si vous pouvez utiliser des illustrations. Lesquelles? Comment pourrez-vous les utiliser?

5 Commencez maintenant à organiser/structurer votre exposé. Dans quel ordre allez-vous parler des aspects différents? Ecrivez une liste de tous les aspects que vous allez couvrir.

6 Préparez bien le langage que vous allez utiliser; pensez à des façons différentes de dire la même chose. Préparez des définitions des mots difficiles.

7 Regardez vos notes pour voir si votre exposé pourrait bénéficier d'aides visuelles (feuilles transparentes pour le rétroprojecteur, une carte de la région, etc). Fabriquez-les.

8 Ecrivez des notes sous chaque rubrique - avec elles, indiquez les illustrations/diapos à utiliser. Montrez ces notes à votre professeur la veille de votre exposé.

---

*Ressources de soutien no 2: Liste de documents - la Normandie*

**Vous avez choisi LA NORMANDIE. Voici la liste de documents à votre disposition:**

| | | |
|---|---|---|
| 1 | Livres | La France (atlas)<br>La Normandie - Pays et Gens (Larousse)<br>La Tapisserie de Bayeux |
| 2 | Article(s) de journal | Autour des régions (Le Point) |
| 3 | Enregistrements | Aperçus sur la Normandie (cassette no 340) |
| 4 | Vidéos | Les plages du débarquement et la bataille de Normandie (vidéo no 39) |
| 5 | Diapositives | Normandie côte et campagne (diapos no 64) |

**N'oubliez pas que ces documents coûtent très cher, et d'autres étudiants en ont besoin. Veuillez les remettre dans l'endroit correct après les avoir utilisés.**

*Agree/disagree/ negotiate/persuade/ counter arguments/ express a variety of emotions and feelings*

Some of the new syllabuses already contain tests in the oral examination in which candidates have to negotiate or persuade - a kind of advanced role-play. This type of practical activity based on situations which students may potentially encounter is likely to play an increasingly important part in oral assessment; if there is to be a closing of the gap between the 'academic' 'A' level and the vocational BTEC style of work, then assignment-based work will grow, and with it oral tasks of a practical nature. At the same time, the more traditional style of discussion is likely to continue to feature in 'A' level oral tests, whether in a summative examination or within the context of periodic assessment. Classroom activities which encourage students to develop the interactive skills of discussion, debate, argument and negotiation therefore serve the needs of a wide range of students in a variety of potential contexts. The sample included here contains ideas for small-group work which can be used at various stages of the 'A' level course. In every case there is an objective to be achieved, an outcome to be decided or negotiated, and this is a key element where discussion is to take place. It is possible to ask students to engage in open-ended discussion on a given topic for a limited period of time, but unless there is a reason for that discussion, it is likely to be aimless and less effective.

## Exercice 51

*Comment persuader ... le vélo ou le bus?*

**Groupe A:**

**Vous êtes très sportif/sportive. Vous avez décidé d'aller en vacances avec votre copain(e) cet été en Bretagne. Mais votre copain tient à prendre l'autobus/le car, tandis que vous préféreriez faire du vélo. Préparez tous les arguments que vous pourriez utiliser pour essayer de l'en persuader. Imaginez les arguments qu'il/elle pourrait utiliser et trouvez des réponses.**

[10 minutes]

**Groupe B:**

**C'est vous qui préférez prendre le bus ou le car pour les vacances en Bretagne. Préparez tous les arguments possibles pour soutenir votre point de vue et pour persuader votre copain(e) de tous les avantages de faire cela.**

[10 minutes]

**Après, la classe se divise en paires avec un membre de chaque groupe. Vous avez 7 minutes pour arriver à une décision, sinon vous devrez accompagner votre famille chez les grand'parents!**

***Exercise 51*** *shows how a brief negotiating activity can be structured. The subject is quite straightforward and could be integrated into a topic on leisure, ideal in the first few weeks of an 'A' level course, since it relates closely to students' own experience and is not too demanding in terms of vocabulary or ideas. Features likely to contribute to a successful outcome are: preparation of ideas and language in larger groups (though any larger than five and there is the danger of the less confident contributing nothing); a realistic task; clear time limits; a clear objective. Some or all of these techniques can be used throughout the course.*

## Exercice 52

*Travail oral à trois [10 minutes]*

**Première personne:** **Vous allez à l'agence de vacances pour vous renseiger sur des vacances actives pour vous et votre famille. Vous avez tous fait du cheval, mais vous préférez des randonnées à pied ou peut-être le canoë-kayak. Si c'est possible, vous préférez le Midi (Provence/Ardèche/Languedoc?). Quand l'agent essaie de vous persuader d'acheter des vacances équestres en Auvergne, vous suggérez toutes sortes de difficultés avec ce genre de vacances.**

**Deuxième personne:** **Vous êtes agent de vacances et vous essayez de persuader votre client(e) d'acheter des vacances équestres en Auvergne - bien que ce ne soit pas son choix préféré. Quand il/elle pose des difficultés, vous faites tout votre possible pour montrer que ses anxiétés ne sont pas bien fondées; vous devez donc le/la convaincre de prendre ces vacances.**

**Troisième personne:** **Vous êtes observateur/observatrice. A la fin des 10 minutes, vous devez décider si vous êtes convaincu(e) par le client (qui ne veut pas vraiment prendre ces vacances équestres) ou l'agent. Qui a utilisé les arguments les plus convaincants? Expliquez et justifiez votre choix à la classe.**

[Cette activité peut être faite avec une variété de vacances: la moitié du groupe préparera des brochures différentes, pour vendre 'leurs' vacances à des clients; le reste de la classe sera des représentants de familles avec des intérêts et besoins divers.]

*The kind of preparatory work suggested in Exercise 51 can be done in groups before students are asked to carry out the role-play in* ***Exercise 52****. In any case, they will/may need some help with the language of seeking information, polite refusal, etc. This can either be provided by the teacher on a sheet, or can be arrived at by pooling of ideas before the start of the exercise. The new feature is the use of an observer, whose role is to listen to the arguments and make a final decision about who has won the debate. To ensure that observers are actively involved, they must be required to report back to the class on their decision.*

## Exercice 53

*Travail oral de groupe (pour des classes plus nombreuses)*

**Faites une reconstruction du procès de Meursault. Les membres de la classe prendront les rôles différents. Pour ce travail, il faut bien préparer votre rôle à l'avance. Ordre suggéré:**

**1 Distribution des rôles:**

Meursault
le procureur
l'avocat de la défense
le juge/président
Marie
Raymond
quelques membres du jury
le directeur de l'asile

[on pourrait peut-être se passer de ces personnages si la classe n'est pas assez nombreuse]

( Salamano)
( Masson)
( Céleste)
( le concierge de l'asile)

**2 Préparation des rôles (devoirs)**

**3 Le procès** (la durée d'une leçon?)

- interrogation de Meursault par le procureur/la défense
- interrogation des témoins par le procureur/la défense
- réquisitions du procureur et de la défense (chacune 2-3 minutes)

**4 Débat du jury avec leur jugement**

***Exercise 53*** *is much more demanding, requiring first of all a good understanding of the text of L'Etranger in all its detail and an appreciation of the characters and their motivation. Because it involves everyone in the class and has a critical outcome, it can be an exciting vehicle for oral work. Time limits need to be set for each section of the trial. Students should be encouraged to do the casting themselves - they are aware of their own limitations and will respond much better than if the teacher allocates the roles.*

## Exercice 54

*Travail oral à deux*

**(a) Avec votre partenaire, considérez les adjectifs suivants. Dans quelle mesure est-il possible de dire que chacun est une bonne description de la vie montagnarde décrite dans le texte? Pour chacun vous devez dire si, l'adjectif ne *convient pas* [0], *convient peu* [1], est *assez convenable* [2], ou *très convenable* [3].**

**Soyez prêt(e) à justifier et à défendre vos décisions devant la classe.**

| | 0 | 1 | 2 | 3 |
|---|---|---|---|---|
| juste | | | | |
| équilibrée | | | | |
| heureuse | | | | |
| simple | | | | |
| dure | | | | |
| monotone | | | | |
| riche | | | | |
| terrible | | | | |
| solitaire | | | | |
| bien réglée | | | | |
| sauvage | | | | |

**(b) Reconsidérez la liste. Lequel de tous les adjectifs donnés serait le plus apte à décrire la vie montagnarde? (Vous ne pouvez en choisir qu'un seul! Si vous préférez, vous pouvez choisir un adjectif qui n'est pas dans la liste.) Vous avez 5 minutes pour vous décider.**

L'adjectif choisi: ________________

***Exercise 54*** *(like Exercises 55 and 56) involves consideration of a number of different aspects or ideas relating to a topic, and therefore presupposes the ability to compare and prioritise. Where a list of items is presented in this way, it is important that students learn to give proper thought and attention to each item. The danger is to reach rapid decisions on each in an attempt to get to the end of the list. The exercise is very clearly structured, though obviously allows the stronger students to develop and justify their ideas.*

## Exercice 55

*Trouvez la peine qui convient*

**En groupes de deux ou trois discutez les incidents ci-dessous. Dans chaque cas trouvez la sanction qui vous semble être juste, morale et efficace.**

(a) Meurtre d'une vieille dame et vol de ses économies.

(b) Bagarre dans la rue après un match de foot - un jeune passant blessé.

(c) Holdup armé à la banque. Aucun blessé.

(d) Le vieillard tue son agresseur.

(e) Viol d'une petite fille.

(f) Une femme tue son mari sadique.

(g) Des mineurs s'attaquent à la police pendant une manifestation.

(h) Un fou tire sur la foule au supermarché.

(i) Bavure policière. Un agent tue un manifestant à coups de matraque.

(j) Emeute de jeunes immigrés. Magasins saccagés, passants blessés, un policier mort.

(k) Explosion dans un grand magasin - 53 morts.

(l) Un homme tue son voisin à cause du bruit.

**Donnez vos conclusions à toute la classe.**

***Exercise 55*** *is more open-ended in that no penalties are suggested and much more subtle discussions can take place on the nature of the qualifying factors. The reporting-back session is likely to throw up some violently conflicting opinions.*

## Exercice 56

*Travail oral de groupe (préparé individuellement)*
*Exposition de l'art francais*

(a) *Travail individuel (10 minutes):*

**Vous travaillez dans un musée et on vous a demandé de choisir 8 tableaux impressionnistes. Ces tableaux repésenteront ce qu'il y a de mieux dans le mouvement impressionniste, dans le cadre d'une exposition sur l'art français en général. Quels tableaux choisiriez-vous? Mettez-les en ordre de priorité.**

| PEINTRE | TABLEAU |
|---|---|
| 1 | |
| 2 | |
| 3 | |
| 4 | |
| 5 | |
| 6 | |
| 7 | |
| 8 | |

(b) *Travail de groupe à 3 ou à 4 (20-30 minutes):*

**Vous faites partie d'un comité qui décide sur le contenu de l'exposition. Mettez-vous d'accord sur les huit tableaux que vous allez exposer!**

***Exercise 56*** *presents a format which is ideal for exploitation at the end of a topic. It presumes a considerable amount of knowledge and the ability to describe pictures, as well as the capacity to assess 'value' or 'importance' of a painting. In such activities the students should be trained to treat the individual decision-making phase as an important one in preparing ideas and arguments. The second phase (group decision-making) provides them, eventually, with important skills for life: careful listening, modifying views, persuasion, argument and prioritising. Once students have done this kind of activity a couple of times (and can be trusted to talk in French), they are best left to get on with the group discussions entirely on their own. A teacher 'listening in' is likely to be more harmful than constructive. This kind of oral work is the culmination of all the others - though variations of it can be introduced reasonably early in the course, provided the decisions to be reached are appropriate to the topic in question.*

## KEY POINTS

- The objectives of the 'A' level course for speaking are principally:

    - to develop the ability to pronounce the language correctly
    - to achieve reasonable accuracy in expressing oneself
    - to exchange and communicate information
    - to summarise texts
    - to express and develop ideas and opinions
    - to agree/disagree/negotiate/persuade/counter arguments/express a variety of emotions and feelings

- Future syllabuses will probably see growth in periodic assessment covering a range of oral activities
- Communication in French should be seen as normal in class
- Regular small-group work is essential, but groupings should vary if possible
- Most successful speaking takes place after input of language/ideas
- Clearly-defined, attainable tasks help build confidence
- Feedback on oral work is best done privately
- General class oral work should be limited - only the strong likely to perform
- Some types of oral activity are best done with the teacher not listening
- Pair work should always be designed to give both partners a role
- Discussions/presentations/extended oral work need gradual build-up with more specific and limited exercises
- Students need to develop the skill of using brief notes from which to talk
- Full-scale French exposés by individual students require thorough support and guided preparation
- Group participation in individual *exposés* needs fostering
- Oral activities should have an aim or outcome
- Whatever the exercise, students need to be fed appropriate enabling language

# Chapter 5
# DEVELOPING WRITING

The reason this skill has been left until last is quite deliberate. It is the one which is best developed as the culmination of work in the other three skills and is likely to be carried out most successfully after the thorough groundwork of reading texts has been accomplished. Only when vocabulary, ideas and new structures have all been assimilated in this way, confirmed and extended perhaps through listening material, then finally practised and further expanded in oral activities, can the student write with confidence - at least when it comes to more extended forms of writing. However, with a mixed-skill approach, it is of course quite possible and desirable that 'micro-writing' (see below) will take place at various stages along the continuum.

Although written coursework clearly encompasses most of the other types of writing and is not in itself a different type, a specific section of the chapter will be devoted to a brief analysis of some of the issues and problems related to it, since it is a feature of the newer 'A' level syllabuses in which teachers may not have experience.

Surprisingly, in view of the lower profile of writing in GCSE and the perception of the new 'A' levels as vehicles for a higher profile of spoken French, the demands being made on 'A' level candidates are actually greater in the new syllabuses in this field. Candidates now have to write longer essays, coursework loads can be quite heavy, and essays on the literature (when selected) are now in the foreign language. Furthermore, early evidence from work produced for the new 'A' levels demonstrates a marked improvement in overall quality, though sadly the writing tasks students are obliged to perform are still largely traditional and academic, and only rarely relate to real-life tasks which would prove practically useful to them at some later stage. Even pieces of coursework, in which there is usually scope for personal selection when it comes to both form and content, nearly always conform to the standard essay format.

## Objectives

As for speaking, the criteria used to assess performance in the longer writing component(s) of the examination varies in quantity and precision from board to board. Again, some syllabuses contain a range of grids relating to specific aspects of performance, whilst others adopt a more holistic approach, giving broad definitions to describe bands of performance, and including reference to a number of different factors within each band (e.g. grammar, fluency, vocabulary). For shorter pieces, or micro-writing, the criteria will vary considerably, depending on the nature of the task. Invariably, though, there will be an element of the marks for accuracy and one for 'quality of language'. The objectives, grouped according to the contexts within which they are likely to be required, might be defined as follows:

★ be able to write accurately in very brief structured contexts, e.g. answer questions, re-phrase, define words and expressions, paraphrase, complete sentences (W1)

(see *Micro-writing*)

★ be able to:
- write fluently and naturally in response to a passage or passages (normally in the foreign language) (W2)
- write accurately (W3)
- use a variety of linguistic structures (W4)
- show knowledge of a range of appropriate vocabulary (W5)
- carry out the task effectively (W6)
- show understanding of the stimulus passage(s) (W7)
- structure the writing appropriately (W8)

(see *Guided/responsive writing*)

★ be able to:
- write fluently and naturally on prepared topics (W2)
- write accurately (W3)
- use a variety of linguistic structures (W4)
- show knowledge of a range of appropriate vocabulary (W5)
- produce a relevant answer (W6)
- develop and expand ideas/opinions (W9)
- support argument by detailed knowledge (W10)
- structure the essay appropriately (W8)

(see *Discursive essay*)

★ (In addition to producing language and content appropriate to the form - whether discursive or non-discursive - as above) be able to:
- work independently (W11)
- use research skills (W12)
- present the coursework appropriately (W13)

(see *Written coursework*)

**Contexts**

In most cases, then, the target is to be able to write in the foreign language within the following four contexts:

★ micro-writing
★ guided/responsive/non-discursive writing (e.g. letter, article, brochure, report)
★ discursive essay
★ written coursework

Very occasionally, in the context of either coursework or 'non-discursive' writing, a student will produce a piece of imaginative writing (e.g. short story or dialogue). Although this can produce surprisingly good results in the more imaginative students and is something which students tend to enjoy, the occurrence of this kind of writing at 'A' level is not felt to be sufficiently common to merit specific treatment here.

**Further guidelines**

Because writing is the least ephemeral of the skills and can be analysed more easily at leisure, there has been a tendency to treat it as the easiest to assess and deal with. Nonetheless, two-year courses should aim to develop the skill gradually and not fall into the trap of asking too much too soon, through mere habit. A planned development of writing skills should therefore take the following into account:

- **Relationship between reading and writing**

Writing is the culmination of much input, in terms of content and language. It can only be developed adequately by training students to read, digest and then imitate. Students will need much help in identifying useful material in texts, then using it without copying too much.

- **Appropriateness of tasks**

Concentrate in the early part of the course on writing at the 'micro' level (phrases, sentences, brief sections), but allow students some flexibility to express themselves at greater length as soon as they are ready. In the first year, extended writing might be limited to guided writing exercises, in which a good deal of help is given to students by means of texts, discussions, etc. These should cover different formats to extend their skills in a variety of contexts.

- **Importance of paragraph-writing**

The basis for good essays is good paragraphs: it is important to develop the ability to write in paragraph form before writing full-length essays.

- **Enabling language**

Support written tasks with enabling language. This is as important in writing as it is in speaking, but tends to be neglected.

- **Proper correction of work**

Ensure that written exercises on reading and listening texts are corrected accurately, without insisting on accuracy at the expense of all else.

## Developing the skills

### *Micro-writing*

The kind of writing being referred to here is that which occurs in very brief, well-defined contexts, but where the quality of the writing itself is being tested either in addition to or separate from any element of content/comprehension. (The writing which asks students to respond in French **merely to show comprehension** and which is not marked for accuracy or quality of language, does not fall into this category.) Thus, any form of brief writing at the level of word, phrase, sentence or beyond, but where structure or development does not play a part could be termed micro-writing. Some of the newer syllabuses have included in their testing a paper or section which might be referred to as *'Use of language'*. This usually includes manipulation exercises of an unspecified nature, cloze tests, re-phrasing, completion of sentences and so on. Such exercises have largely been introduced as a replacement to the prose, to test use of language and accuracy in a very closely defined context, but without recourse to the mother tongue. They have proved to be successful in testing such skills and students and teachers have generally enjoyed this kind of format, but some teachers are unhappy about the inauthentic nature of the tests and would prefer to see written language tested in more realistic contexts. Some boards have attempted to achieve this by introducing carefully crafted exercises, often in a mixed-skill approach. But however diverse the boards' offerings may be in terms of micro-writing, the skill is fundamental to the development of more extended forms of writing (discursive and non-discursive) and should be part of normal classroom practice.

The importance of using reading passages as a source for the development of writing skills has already been stressed in *Developing reading: acquiring grammatical/syntactical knowledge* (p 45), but there could obviously be an overlap with other areas; wherever language is produced **and** the quality assessed, one could say that the skill of micro-writing is being developed (e.g. Exercises 4 [definitions], 10 [cloze], 11 [grid completion]). In the original contexts in which these exercises were used, it was not the intention to assess quality of language, since they were designed principally to develop comprehension/reading skills; however, they would automatically help develop writing skills from the moment that accuracy or quality came into play. In most situations, teachers would use these exercises as a tool for extending reading **and** writing skills. Although the development of the various skills has been artificially separated for the purposes of our analysis, it is important that students be encouraged to think in terms of their mutual dependency, otherwise we shall merely be substituting one form of fragmented course for another.

However, if one uses the exercises referred to above principally or partially as language exercises, one will need to bear in mind a number of points, viz:

- To consolidate accuracy, students will need to see the 'correct' answers written (but see Chapter 7 on *Assessment and monitoring*). OHPs with the answers are an ideal solution, eliminating the need to take all work in.

- In many instances, there will be no right or wrong answer: the skill lies in producing an acceptable, accurate version, or one which fits the grammatical as well as the sense context.

- For Question and Answer and grid completion exercises, students should always be encouraged to re-phrase or express the original passage in their own words wherever possible; copying the correct section of the passage may be adequate to begin with, but writing skills can only properly be developed by a degree of independence.

- In definition exercises, the requirements of the examination will be constrained by the board's policy on dictionary use. Boards which do not allow use of a monolingual dictionary may well set exercises on an individual word. Others will, for obvious reasons, be limited to the re-wording of phrases or expressions. But whatever the policy, the skill of defining words without recourse to the dictionary is one to be fostered.

- The relationship between oral skills and micro-writing should be particularly close since the need for the teacher to explain words and phrases/ask for definitions from the students is central to communicating in the foreign language. If it is a regular part of classroom activity, it should automatically lead to a strengthening of micro-writing skills. As examples of the type of exercise used to develop micro-writing have already been used in other contexts, it is not considered necessary to add any further examples here.

*Guided/responsive/ non-discursive writing*

Whilst some of the features of language fostered by micro-writing will inevitably be found in writing of the kind needed in guided/ responsive/non-discursive contexts, there are two distinctive features of the latter not to be found in micro-writing: structure/form (and therefore presumably some sense of development) and content related to stimulus passages or other topic-centred material. This form of writing is not directly related to length, since relatively short pieces may fall within it as being legitimate kinds of responsive writing. All the writing which goes beyond micro-writing but does not fall into the category of the discursive essay belongs here. There will naturally be some grey areas; paragraph-writing could be 'non-discursive' or 'discursive' in kind, depending on its presumed purpose, but all forms of extended writing which do not fit into the traditional essay mould could be termed 'non-discursive'. Since students are often given a free rein in coursework, their writing often turns out to be non-discursive. And given that there is an undercurrent away from some of the more 'academic' forms of testing, it is quite possible that we shall see a gradual move away from traditional essay writing towards forms which are more common in everyday usage (e.g. the writing of reports, summaries, perhaps letters). 'Guided writing' refers to those types of exercise to be found in one or two new syllabuses in which material is given to candidates in the form of ideas/a text and a format is suggested for them to use/develop/respond to that material. In some cases, the exemplar material will include the appropriate stimulus material or exercises in other skill areas which act as a build-up to the writing.

## Exercice 57

*Travail oral et écrit à deux*

**Durée: 1 heure**

**Avec votre partenaire, produisez une affiche visée aux touristes dans les parcs nationaux. La taille dépendra du papier/carton disponible. Le sujet doit être *une représentation du Code de bonne conduite*. Vous pouvez selectionner autant de règles que vous voulez parmi les neuf.**

- Il doit y avoir un minimum de 100 mots
- Utilisez des illustrations/dessins pour rendre l'affiche plus attrayante
- Réfléchissez bien aux titres/sous-titres etc

**A la fin, tout le monde votera pour décider de l'affiche gagnante.**

***Exercise 57** is an example of a form of guided writing which goes down well with students in the first two or three terms of their 'A' level course - the production of a poster. The exercise presupposes the study of a text or brochure about national parks which will have given students some ideas about public behaviour in them. Imperative forms are an obvious linguistic point to revise beforehand. The quality of the artwork is likely to vary enormously, depending on students' abilities and resources available, but visually exciting pieces are often produced and can lead to a discussion on techniques of persuasion. The brevity of the written language required should encourage the consideration of density of language - how best to express the maximum/the important in an effective way. A variation on this which focuses more on the writing and less on the graphics is to give students a card/poster with designs/illustrations already on it and ask them to provide appropriate commentary. Posters and other exercises with a visual element lend themselves to classroom display; sixth formers deserve to be encouraged in their work as much as younger learners, and a supportive and changing classroom environment is a good aid to motivation. If any correction of the work is to be done, it should be done on the reverse, so as not to spoil the visual effect or create negative feelings about the display.*

## Exercice 58

Ce que Sisley recherchait dans ses paysages, c'était une certaine organisation de l'espace : son sens de la construction, qu'il avait probablement hérité de Corot, l'amenait à respecter l'étagement des différents plans. Aussi la route se perdant à l'horizon constitua-t-elle l'un des thèmes privilégiés du peintre, sans cesse récurrent dans son œuvre. Souvent, c'est elle qui relie le premier plan au lointain et qui contribue à « trouer » l'espace, d'où des effets de perspective très réussis.

Cette illusion de la troisième dimension est particulièrement spectaculaire lorsque la route s'en va perpendiculairement à la surface du tableau : afin d'accentuer l'impression de profondeur, l'artiste a alors osé des raccourcis audacieux, ainsi pour représenter les arbres qui scandent *Le chemin de la Machine à Louveciennes*. Un jeu de lignes s'établit grâce aux verticales des fûts reprises par les horizontales de leurs ombres. Sisley a souvent pris soin d'humaniser ses paysages en y introduisant quelques petites figures à la manière de Jongkind. Enfin, il a judicieusement utilisé la montée que le chemin connaît à cet endroit pour créer un point de fuite légèrement décentré et obtenir une vue plongeante sur l'arrière-plan ensoleillé.

Alfred SISLEY (1839–1899)

*Le chemin de la Machine à Louveciennes*, dit aussi
*La route, vue du chemin de Sèvres* 1873

(a) *Travail à deux:*

**Comment parler de la composition d'un tableau? Sisley a mené des recherches de perspective dans ses tableaux. Lisez d'abord ce commentaire sur *Le chemin de la Machine à Louveciennes* (1873). Avec votre partenaire soulignez tous les mots (verbes, adverbes, substantifs, adjectifs) qui portent sur la construction du tableau et faites-en des listes, en suivant les exemples donnés.**

| VERBES | ADVERBES | SUBSTANTIFS | ADJECTIFS |
|---|---|---|---|
| relier à | perpendiculairement | profondeur | plongeant(e) |

(b) *Travail écrit:*

**Choisissez encore un tableau de Sisley et essayez d'en décrire la composition en employant autant du vocabulaire ci-dessus que possible.**

*__Exercise 58__ shows how textual study (in this case focusing first on the use of vocabulary to describe the construction of a painting) can be linked directly to responsive writing. Where students are asked to write freely, they should always be given an indication of length, in number of words or, as here, a space to fill up. The problem of marking/correcting can be tackled in different ways. Sometimes the students can be asked to produce writing in class in small groups; if this is done on OHP transparencies, the various versions can be looked at together, emphasising the qualities of each where possible. Or, the work can be taken in and corrected individually. It is important that students receive some feedback and guidance if progress is to be made.*

## Exercice 59

**Vous êtes le patron du bureau où Meursault travaille, et de temps en temps vous ajoutez des détails au dossier de chacun de vos employés. Puisque le dernier rapport sur Meursault a été fait il y a quelque temps, vous décidez d'en écrire un autre qui contient des détails/observations plus récents. Ecrivez donc 100-150 mots sur Meursault ...**

- **ses qualités/défauts comme employé/collègue**
- **vos observations sur son caractère**

> ***Exercise 59*** *is a piece of writing of similar length to the last but more demanding; it requires powers of analysis based on an understanding of the text and gives licence to a certain amount of imagination. Although purists tend to be cynical about this form of imaginative response to literature, many consider it to be a legitimate way of encouraging response in the foreign language (old-style literary criticism is too demanding at this level) and it still demands a sensitive understanding of the book.*

## Exercice 60

**Dans le dernier chapitre, Meursault avoue ne pas avoir pensé depuis bien longtemps à Marie. Imaginez qu'il décide de lui écrire une dernière lettre après la visite de l'aumônier. Rédigez cette lettre ... (250-300 mots).**

> ***Exercise 60*** *is another example of personal/imaginative response to literature, but this time in the non-discursive form of a letter. The length can be varied as appropriate, but should not normally exceed the requirements of a potential examination question or a piece of coursework. This type of extended writing will only draw out good responses after full study of the complete text. The extent to which it should be specifically prepared in class will vary according to the purpose of the piece. Small groups could be asked, for instance, to consider different aspects of the exercise; Meursault's stated feelings for Marie, his state of mind at this point, style/language. It makes sense to give students as much support and guidance as possible in advance, rather than telling them afterwards 'how it should have been done', since this increases confidence and enhances performance.*

## Exercice 61

*Discussion de groupe: Accepter ou ne pas accepter le projet hydraulique de la haute Romanche*

**Divisez la classe en quatre groupes.**

*(a) Travail de préparation (10-15 minutes):*

**Groupe A:** **Vous êtes des <u>représentants de l'EDF</u>. Préparez tous les arguments que vous pourriez utiliser dans une enquête publique pour soutenir le projet de la haute Romanche.**

**Groupe B:** **Vous êtes des <u>gardes-moniteurs</u> dans le Parc national des Ecrins. Préparez tous les arguments que vous pourriez utiliser - surtout en matière d'environnement - dans une enquête publique pour opposer le projet de la haute Romanche.**

**Groupe C:** **Vous êtes de <u>vieux habitants</u> de la vallée de la Romanche, travaillant dans l'agriculture et vous voulez préserver le patrimoine et la vie de votre région avec toutes ses traditions. Préparez donc tous les arguments que vous pourriez utiliser dans une enquête publique pour opposer le projet de la haute Romanche.**

**Groupe D:** **Vous êtes de <u>jeunes habitants</u> de la vallée de la Romanche prêts à partir à la recherche d'emplois, puisque la région n'en a pas. Vous pensez que la région est morte et que le projet pourrait apporter un renouveau de la vie et de l'économie. Préparez tous les arguments que vous pourriez employer dans une enquête publique pour soutenir le projet de la haute Romanche.**

*(b) L'enquête (20 minutes environ):*

**Reformez des groupes de 4 personnes, cette fois avec un représentant de chacun des groupes A, B, C et D. Après, vous avez 20 minutes pour débattre la question.**

*(c) Travail écrit:*

**Vous jouez toujours le rôle de la personne (A, B, C ou D) ci-dessus. Ecrivez une lettre au Courrier des Ecrins pour souligner votre point de vue et pour essayer de convaincre les lecteurs de la justice de votre cause (350 mots maximum).**

*More extended oral activities of the kind to be found in parts (a) and (b) of* ***Exercise 61*** *[cf* ***Exercise 56****] are excellent preparatory grounds for writing. Part (a) enables students to amass ideas and arguments to support their debating powers. The language they use and hear will provide them with just the kind of vocabulary and structures they will need to write the letter in (c). Normally, the written task will be done for homework, but it should be clearly limited in time (say an hour) and set as soon after the oral activity as possible to maximise the carry-over effect.*

*Discursive essay*

The writing of discursive essays has always been a traditional part of 'A' level French syllabuses; it is therefore one with which teachers are highly familiar and at home. However, some changes have been introduced by the new syllabuses and it would be unwise to leave the development of this skill to chance. There are two main differences. Whereas formerly the essays were 'unprepared', covering topics of general interest, perhaps including a choice of discursive and non-discursive, the broad areas of the topics to be set are now outlined in advance, though the particular slant of the questions will not normally be known before the examination. The thinking behind this is that students are much more likely to perform to their best ability if they can write on subjects they have studied. They will have knowledge and detailed information on which to base their answers, as well as the subject-specific language. The second significant development is that more detailed assessment criteria are being used and are available to teachers and students. Although some boards still use simplified grids, the trend is to separate out performance in different areas of content and language. Since performance is likely to vary, this seems a more accurate way of assessing. The consequence of this is that students should be able to prepare themselves more thoroughly by developing specifically those skills defined by the boards.

It has already been suggested that full-length discursive essays should not be attempted early in the 'A' level course, and should probably not be tackled much before the second year. This is to allow time for the gradual development of writing skills in the more closely defined contexts of micro- and guided writing. Some features of discursive writing will automatically form part of this. Other features may be developed throughout this first year (and beyond) without need for recourse to the writing of full essays.

*Exercises 17-19* (shown in *Developing reading*) will increase and consolidate grammatical knowledge; *Exercises 20-21* are designed to help students improve their style, whether in terms of choice of language or structure of sentences. *Exercise 22* sharpens awareness of the structure of texts and paragraphs. All these aspects of writing will contribute to the formation of sound foundations for the students' own writing when it comes to essays. And although one might optimistically imagine that these fundamental skills can and should be taught and acquired early on, in practice they will need reinforcement and consolidation throughout the course.

As specific preparation for the writing of discursive essays, work needs to be done at two levels - the paragraph and the essay itself - and the exercises in this section relate exclusively to such work.

## Exercice 62

*La structure des paragraphes - travail écrit*

1 **(a) Les phrases suivantes constituent un paragraphe - mais elles sont dans le désordre. Remettez-les dans le bon ordre.**

A D'un côté, il y a des régions qui ont la population plus dense et la plus urbanisée, qui voient leur population augmenter.

B Généralement, ce sont les régions centrales de la France qui souffrent des plus grandes pertes de population.

C La densité majeure de la population à travers la France métropolitaine est de 104 habitants par kilomètre carré, mais ce chiffre déguise les vastes différences entre les régions et entre les départements.

D La conclusion majeure tirée de l'analyse des données recueillies est qu'il existe un déséquilibre entre les régions.

E D'un autre côté, il y a ces régions qui sont les moins peuplées et qui connaissent un ralentissement de la croissance de leurs populations et parfois un déclin de leurs populations.

F A une extrémité il y a la Lozère, qui a moins de 20 habitants par kilomètre carré, et à l'autre extrémité on trouve Paris avec 200-400 habitants par kilomètre carré.

| 1 | 2 | 3 | 4 | 5 | 6 |
|---|---|---|---|---|---|
| | | | | | |

**(b) Chaque phrase dans un paragraphe remplit une fonction. Quelles sont les fonctions remplies par les 6 phrases ci-dessus? Choisissez les fonctions dans la liste suivante:**

1 exemple, illustration
2 détails qui appuient un argument/point de vue
3 explication
4 développement d'une idée
5 introduction d'une idée
6 comparaison/contraste
7 résumé
8 conclusion
9 __________ (autre)

| A | B | C | D | E | F |
|---|---|---|---|---|---|
| | | | | | |

**2 (a) Faites la même chose avec les phrases suivantes:**

# *Gaz naturel: une richesse insoupçonnée!*

A Avec plus de 110,000 milliards de $m^3$ de réserves prouvées, la planète peut dormir tranquille.

B Ainsi les réserves prouvées de gaz naturel ne représentaient que 50% des réserves de pétrole en 1970.

C Plus abondant que le pétrole, le gaz naturel est une source d'énergie à la fois propre et fiable.

D De plus, ces réserves ne cessent d'augmenter, grâce aux nouvelles découvertes.

E Presque par hasard, en somme, mais le hasard fait bien les choses.

F Ceci n'est d'ailleurs pas le résultat d'une prospection effrénée.

G Ces réserves représentent aujourd'hui 60 ans de consommation au rythme actuel, alors que les réserves prouvées de pétrole représentent aujourd'hui 30 ans de consommation.

H 'On trouve souvent du gaz naturel en cherchant du pétrole', explique un spécialiste.

| 1 | 2 | 3 | 4 | 5 | 6 | 7 | 8 |
|---|---|---|---|---|---|---|---|
| | | | | | | | |

**(b) Et pour les fonctions, choisissez encore dans la liste en bas de la page 112.**

| A | B | C | D | E | F | G | H |
|---|---|---|---|---|---|---|---|
| | | | | | | | |

**(c) Maintenant, écrivez un paragraphe de 90-110 mots au sujet de l'énergie solaire.**

**(d) Quelles sont les fonctions de chacune des phrases de votre paragraphe?**

| | | | | | | | |
|---|---|---|---|---|---|---|---|
| | | | | | | | |

**Exercise 62** *helps make students aware of the internal structure of paragraphs. By focusing on the function of different sentences students should learn to develop their own ideas in paragraph form. However, it is important to apply this exercise to all kinds of paragraphs, so that they do not become too fixed in their writing. Here, two examples are given, then students write their own paragraph and analyse the function of the sentences they have written.*

## Exercice 63

**Ecrivez un seul paragraphe d'environ 120 mots qui résume les idées dans le texte ci-dessous sur l'exode rural, commençant avec la phrase suivante:**

'Si on étudie le Livradois-Forez, on voit bien que l'exode rural a eu des répercussions importantes ...'

**[Ces mots ne sont pas compris dans les 120 mots!]**

### L'exode et ses répercussions

L'exode qui a frappé la région à partir de la fin du siècle dernier et qui a fait perdre à celle-ci les deux tiers de sa population a donc eu pour conséquences un appauvrissement et une dégradation de ces milieux, tout aussi graves que celles qu'entraîne la surpopulation ou la surfréquentation dans d'autres régions ; et les exemples venant à l'appui de cette affirmation sont nombreux :

- les anciennes "hautes chaumes" du Forez sont devenues en quelques années des landes à "bruyères" denses et dont le cortège floristique est considérablement appauvri alors que le pâturage traditionnel les avait ennoblies.
- la multiplication des plantations anarchiques dites en "timbre-poste", conséquence importante de cet exode, a immobilisé de nombreuses terres agricoles, défiguré des sites, uniformisé les climats locaux (baisse de la température moyenne et de l'ensoleillement, augmentation de l'humidité atmosphérique).
- de nombreux bâtiments et ouvrages traditionnels, témoins de l'originalité et le l'identité régionale (maisons en pisé ou à colombages pour la plaine, vieux ponts, moulins...) tombent en désuétude après le départ des habitants ou perdent leur caractère par des modifications fâcheuses. De même, beaucoup de monuments qui présentent une grande valeur historique ou architecturale se dégradent à un rythme accéléré ( châteaux et gentilhommières).
- enfin, des activités nouvelles, premières réactions à cet exode, entraînant parfois des aménagements irraisonnés, n'ont pas été sans conséquences en ce qui concerne l'environnement (surpâturage ovin, plantation en altitude, certains aménagements touristiques ...). Mais, et c'est peut-être la seule conséquence heureuse du relatif sous-développement régional, le Livradois-Forez n'a pas encore trop souffert de l'urbanisme délirant et des suréquipements destructeurs préconisés dans les années 60 et qui ont cruellement touché certaines régions voisines.

## Exercice 64

*Titres de rédaction (350 mots environ)*

(a) Est-ce que vous pensez que *L'Etranger* pourrait devenir un bon film? Quelles sont les qualités qui seraient accentuées par un film? Quels sont les moments les plus frappants?

(b) 'Un vrai chef-d'oeuvre littéraire reflète les problèmes universels de la vie humaine.' Discutez en vous référant à un des livres que vous avez étudiés (ou bien à tous les deux si vous voulez).

(c) D'après vos études, quelles mesures ont été prises en France pour contrôler la violence? Faites une évaluation de leur efficacité.

(d) Quel genre de personne serait le plus particulièrement intéressé par une visite à la région/ville de votre choix: un historien? un peintre? un industriel? un scientifique? quelqu'un d'autre? ou tous? Expliquez votre réponse.

(e) Expliquez les difficultés de choix et d'opinion politiques qui ont confronté le Français moyen pendant l'Occupation.

*__Exercise 63__ is one example of how paragraph writing can be set. In this case, the paragraph is a summary of the content of a longer text, and students are guided in their treatment by being given the first sentence. This contains pointers which need to be developed. Similar paragraph-writing exercises can be used to help students with introductions and conclusions.*

*In the end, however much one prepares students for the individual skills which contribute towards the writing of essays, the only way in which they will complete their development is by writing essays themselves. Indeed, the skill of welding together language and content into a coherent whole is one which needs considerable practice. But although students certainly need practice in doing 'timed' questions under examination conditions, this should be left to the 'mock' examinations and to the very last part of the course (i.e. the last term or so); practice at getting it right and performing well, albeit with preparation and support, is likely to get students into the right habits which should then be easier to transfer to more difficult conditions. The frequency with which one elects to set full essays within the second year will be governed by two important factors: student workload and staff workload! Teachers with experience of topic-based programmes over a number of years have come to the conclusion that there is a real danger of student overload; we should not underestimate the amount of time needed on preparation of texts. Similarly, the increasing demands on staff with coursework, preparation and the application of detailed criteria in assessing written work (for example) will mean that extended pieces of writing of any kind cannot be set too often.*

*How often, then, and under what conditions? The answer depends to some extent on the length of study of topics. Assuming four to five weeks for each topic in the second year, one 'essay' (discursive or non-discursive) per topic is probably enough, though there may be shorter pieces of writing in between. The conditions will and should vary. If the writing forms part of coursework, the conditions will have been laid down by the board. For other pieces, students could be given a week or so to complete the essay in their own time (with or without other homework, as appropriate). In the second term of the second year, the demands can be increased by giving students notice to prepare a given question which must then be answered in class (without notes! - students are generally not good at knowing when notes end and essays begin!). In the third term, students can be given unprepared questions (though knowing when they will be set and on which topic(s)) since they should be fully prepared for this by now. Obviously, teachers' views about the timing and conditions will vary: the different formats may well be mixed over the year. __Exercise 64__ is simply a list of sample questions on a variety of topics - literary and non-literary - of the kind now popular.*

## Written coursework

Issues affecting planning have already been discussed in Chapter 1, but there are other problems relating to the production of written coursework which are more appropriately placed here, since they are operational rather than strategic.

### ★ What specific preparation is needed for coursework?

Clearly, students need to be able to work independently and carry out the requirements of the coursework within the stipulated regulations. As coursework approaches, it is sensible to discuss fully with students all the issues associated with it, including any anxieties they may have. It is important that they should fully understand its purposes and value as a spin-off on other skills, and essential that the regulations and guidelines provided by the board are explicitly understood. This should be done sympathetically and in a way which does not promote coursework as being more important than it is - namely just one component of their final assessment. If we as teachers have anxieties about it, we should resolve those anxieties and avoid transmitting them to the students.

But what of more long-term preparation? Independent study is not something which students can learn overnight. Nor is it something peculiar to languages. Study habits and curricular practices throughout their education will have prepared students (or not) for this kind of activity. Some will be much more skilled at this stage than others for all kinds of reasons. However, if we as language teachers know that our students will be required to undertake coursework, it is our duty to ensure that we do not throw them in at the deep end and hope that they have already learned to swim elsewhere. Independence can only be properly fostered in an environment where student-centred learning is encouraged. That is fundamentally the reason why, in Chapter 1, it was recommended that individual choice of topics should be permitted if at all possible. There are, though, other ways in which - throughout the course - students can and should be given more autonomy or trained in skills which can help them when they have to be autonomous:

- They should know what reference books are available to them and what use can be made of them. Dictionary use has already been covered, but the same applies to encyclopaedias etc.
- Individualised activities, however short, should be commonplace. These can range from choosing a newspaper article to talk about to the class to researching for a detailed topic presentation. Only by carrying out such activities can they become fully acquainted with the resources at their disposal and learn to select/organise material appropriately.
- They will need specific help with note-taking and/or the selection of appropriate material from texts/recordings.
- Resources will need to be well-organised and accessible (see Chapter 8).
- Personal organisation of time/work and the planning which goes with it should be monitored and developed right from the start.

### ★ How important is the choice of titles?

Where the choice of titles of individual pieces is left to the student/centre it is important not to take the decision lightly. Early experience with coursework on the newer syllabuses suggests that inadequate attention is given to this, with the result that coursework pieces are unfocused, bland and repetitive. Titles tend to be mere labels - *La Normandie, La drogue en France aujourd'hui* - with an all-embracing remit. If more specific wording can be found there is a risk of narrowing down the subject, but this is much more likely to give direction and structure to the piece, produce analysis, but above all lead to coursework which is lively, personal and more interesting to read. If the work is non-discursive in format, then a potential audience should be borne in mind: who is the piece designed for? Does it fulfil its functions? If it is a discursive essay, then it ought to be framed as a question (*Pourquoi la Normandie attire-t-elle tant de visiteurs? La drogue pose-t-elle une menace grave à la société d'aujourd'hui?*)

### ★ How can we be sure the work is not copied/is the student's unaided work?

This is undoubtedly the single question most commonly asked by teachers as they face coursework for the first time. It is a question which covers both the 'lifting' of material from texts and the potential help they may receive from third parties, particularly native speakers - parents, relatives, the assistant(e), French correspondants or just plain friends. Experience so far seems to suggest that if any abuse does occur, it is rare. For one thing, the regulations supplied by boards are explicit and leave no-one in doubt as to the severity of the penalty if abuse is proven. It is our duty as teachers to make this clear to students and to do all in our power to ensure fair play. For another, as teachers we know the work of our students well and are invariably capable of spotting the copying of material, because of its inconsistency either with the rest of the piece or with work normally produced by the student. Similarly, it is usually possible to detect collaboration with a native speaker through unexpected stylistic niceties. And thirdly, through knowledge of the resources available and the bibliography provided, it should be possible to check the source material for purposes of comparison. Clearly, the acquisition and use of language from their texts are techniques which we promote among students during the course: to an extent, it is therefore a desirable practice. What neither the teachers nor the boards want is wholesale copying. The extent to which candidates may use language from the sources is a matter for the boards to define. Ultimately, if we believe in the positive effect of coursework, it is up to us to make it work.

### ★ What is the teacher's role vis-à-vis the coursework itself?

The extent to which help can be given to students by teachers at any stage of the writing of coursework is bound to vary from one board to another, and teachers must abide by those rules. Where help at the planning stage is permitted, it is obviously very much in the student's interest to take advantage of this help. Teachers can suggest ways of improving the plan by, for example, rearranging the order, suggesting additions or deletions, discussing possible ways of developing particular ideas and so on. The important thing is to ensure that there are no major omissions and that the piece is logically constructed. It may also be possible to discuss use of resources and point students to particular source material they may have overlooked. A tendency among them is to produce very skeletal plans; the fuller the plan they can bring for discussion (within the rules) the more profitable the preparation is likely to be.

Where a number of pieces have to be produced as coursework, it is generally the rule that they are marked as they come in (subject to moderation) and feedback can be given to students on the work. If they are allowed to see the piece with marks and corrections, so much the better; it may be quite costly in terms of time to give students proper individual attention both at the planning and at the feedback stages, but the time is well spent and should act as a powerful source of guidance for future work. It can be very fruitful, as follow-up work, to focus on one particular weakness of the coursework piece (in language or content) and get the student to re-write a section remedying the weakness in question. The automatic re-writing of the whole of a coursework piece merely to correct the grammatical mistakes is a tedious and de-motivating task. Far better, for example, to ask them simply to make a list of the gender errors or pinpoint adjectival agreement.

## KEY POINTS

- The objectives of the 'A' level course for writing are:
  - to be able to write accurately in brief, structured contexts
  - to be able to write fluently and accurately in response to a passage on prepared topics
  - to show understanding of a stimulus passage
  - to structure the writing appropriately
  - to be able to use a variety of linguistic structures
  - to show knowledge of a range of appropriate vocabulary
  - to carry out a task effectively
  - to sustain an argument/develop and expand ideas
  - to support an argument by detailed knowledge
  - (for coursework) to develop appropriate research and presentational skills

- Extended writing is the culmination of work in the other skills and should not be attempted early in the course
- Guided writing exercises are most appropriate in the first year
- Writing needs to be developed at the paragraph level before the essay
- Written tasks need supporting with appropriate enabling language
- Reading, listening and speaking exercises can all be used to develop micro-writing skills
- Writing as part of a visual display is worth encouraging
- Writing exercises should normally give an indication of length
- Any free writing should be marked individually
- Personal response tasks tend to be highly motivating
- Extended discussion/debates are an effective form of preparation for writing
- Discursive essays linked to prepared topics generally produce work of a higher quality than 'unprepared' essays
- Extended writing places a heavy burden on students and staff
- Written coursework needs much individual oversight (as allowed) by the teacher - planning, use of resources/time management, etc
- Very careful work and advice is needed by the teacher to ensure students can use textual material appropriately

## Chapter 6

# PRODUCING AN INTEGRATED UNIT

So far the emphasis has been on separate skill development over a period of time. But how can the skills be welded together to form coherent units? And how can one define the content of an individual topic? The answers will depend on a range of factors - amount of syllabus definition, student interest, student progress to date, teacher interest and strengths, the timing of the unit/topic, relationship of the unit/topic to the examination or assessment pattern, etc.

In practical terms, there are likely to be three factors which define the starting point: the topic itself (see Chapter 1), the teaching resources available on that topic, and finally the amount of time which can be devoted to the topic. Although the examination boards do not tend to define the topics very specifically, teachers need to decide on the precise coverage, as this will control which resources to use (if there is a choice!); further decisions will have to be made relating to the order in which to present them and the skills to be developed, bearing in mind (a) the strengths of the resources and (b) the linear development of skills throughout the course.

In order to illustrate the problems raised and how they might be tackled, this chapter will deal specifically with the two aspects of content and skills in relation to one topic: *L'Impressionnisme*. This represents a good compromise between the literary and non-literary and is a subject deeply rooted in French culture. More practically, there is a dossier in the Oxford Delegacy series which is readily available and offers a more than adequate fund of resources for any teacher to use. Some of the raw material in the dossier in the form of texts and tapes has been selected but exploited in a different way.

The chapter begins with a topic summary sheet, identifying the principal objectives in terms of content and skills. Detailed comments on this and the choice, progression and rationale of the exercises are to be found at the foot of each section, but not after each exercise as in previous chapters.

## The topic summary sheet

In order to plan exactly what one is trying to achieve in a given topic, it is helpful to summarise the programme in a tabular form as on the topic summary sheet. At a glance it enables one to see what work is to be covered, in what order and for what purposes. Not only is this helpful to teacher and students when starting the topic, but it can serve as the basis for compiling a complete two-year programme of study. The **Références** refer to the index number allocated to each item which forms part of the resource bank [L = Listening, R = Reading, S = Speaking, W = Writing]. Each of the language objectives (**Buts: Capacités**) is related by a number to the objectives listed in the 'Objectives' sections of Chapters 2-5 (e.g. see p 19). Hence R1 = the first listed objective for Reading, i.e. *Understanding and extending vocabulary and idiom* (see also *Storing/ access/indexing* in Chapter 8; p 163). As such, the sheet can be used as a check for ensuring that all the course objectives in terms of skills have been covered and as the basis for preparing tests. A stand-in teacher can see exactly what work might be done next and how that fits into the overall scheme. The sheet has an important value for students, to whom it should be given at the beginning of the topic. It allows them to obtain relevant materials from the resource bank, and absent students can also use it for catching up on work missed. Many teachers might think that the production of a topic summary sheet of this kind is a difficult and/or time-consuming operation. It need be neither! Summary sheets can be as simple or as detailed as one likes, but the only 'complex' part of them is detailing the *'buts'* for content and skills. As one becomes familiar with the main objectives, this becomes second nature and can be done rapidly. In the early stages of constructing a course of this kind, one might begin simply by listing the title and the resource reference number.

### *Duration and timing*

The purpose of this unit of work is to prepare students for their written examination topic *L'Impressionnisme*. In the examination they will typically have to write an essay of some 300-400 words, but although the general topic can be known, the precise wording of the question is not. They will therefore need to be acquainted with the broad aspects of the topic as well as to know about some of the artists in a fair amount of detail. As an examination topic, its study is situated in the second year of the course (in this case quite early - October) and four to five weeks have been allocated to it. Although the primary objective is to prepare for the essay paper, it should be noted that often the new syllabuses link the oral examination with topics studied, so the ability to speak about the topic is just as crucial. Finally, one should not forget that the purpose of using a multi-skill approach to the topics is to extend **all** the skills, including listening and reading. The unit of work is thus long enough to give students the opportunity to become fully acquainted with the subject matter and to cover a range of materials in differing ways, but without resorting to 'overkill'. At this stage in the course, it is reasonable to expect students to be able to handle texts of a sophisticated nature, and to be able to write a full-length examination essay at the end. If this topic had been placed six months earlier in the course, it would look significantly different, making fewer demands, being shorter in length and being tested in a different way.

## TOPIC SUMMARY SHEET

| SUJET: | L'Impressionnisme | DUREE: | 4-5 semaines | DATE: | Octobre 1990 |
|---|---|---|---|---|---|

| TITRE | REF | BUTS: CONTENU | BUTS: CAPACITES |
|---|---|---|---|
| 1 Travail oral préparatoire | S37 | • Les différentes sortes de peinture<br>• Experiences personnelles de l'art | • Exprimer des opinions (S3)<br>• Parler simplement du contenu d'un tableau (S1) |
| 2 L'Impressionnisme" | R16 | • Origines et détails de l'impressionnisme<br>• Peintres principaux (noms)<br>• Innovations principales | • Apprendre le vocabulaire fondamental de la peinture (R1)<br>• Deviner le sens des mots (R1)<br>• Comprendre globalement (R2)<br>• Exprimer des idées d'une façon différente (W1)<br>• Ecrire avec précision dans un langage assez familier (W2), (W3), (W4), (W5), (W6), (W7), (W8)<br>• Résumer oralement (S2)<br>• Gr: Réviser les temps des verbes (R5,W1) |
| 3 'Quelques influences sur la peinture impressionniste' | L6 | • L'importance de Corot (Monet), estampes japonaises, photographie | • Augmenter le vocabulaire (L1)<br>• Comprendre d'une façon détaillée (L3)<br>• S'exprimer d'une façon précise (W1)<br>• Résumer oralement le contenu d'un passage (S2)<br>• Arriver à des décisions/négocier (S4) |
| 4 'Quand te maries-tu?' | R17 | • Quelques détails concernant l'art et la vie de Gauguin | • Apprendre du vocabulaire technique (R1)<br>• Trouver des renseignements spécifiques dans un texte (R3)<br>• Poser des questions (S1, S2)<br>• Faire des recherches individuelles puis décrire oralement/analyser (S1, S3)<br>• Gr: réviser l'accord des adjectifs |
| 5 'Le choc de l'impressionnisme' | L7 | • La peinture traditionnelle<br>• L'importance du Salon<br>• Les nouvelles valeurs | • Comprendre d'une façon globale (L2) et comprendre d'une façon précise (L3)<br>• Elargir le vocabulaire technique (L1) |

## TOPIC SUMMARY SHEET cont/d

| SUJET: | L'Impressionnisme | DUREE: | 4-5 semaines | | |
|---|---|---|---|---|---|

| TITRE | REF | BUTS: CONTENU | BUTS: CAPACITES |
|---|---|---|---|
| 6 Présentations individuelles sur les artistes | S38 | • La vie et l'oeuvre de peintres impressionnistes sélectionnés<br>• La variété des peintres 'impressionnistes'<br>• L'importance de l'impressionnisme pour l'art moderne | • Faire des recherches individuelles (W11), (W12)<br>• Utiliser des ressources (W12)<br>• Organiser et structurer une présentation<br>• Décrire oralement et analyser (S1,S3)<br>• Réagir/répondre à des questions (S3,S4) |
| 7 'Haro sur Van Gogh et Cézanne' | R18 | • Des vols de tableaux récents<br>• La 'valeur' des tableaux<br>• L'art contre le matérialisme | • Lire rapidement pour repérer des faits (R3) |
| 8 'Exposition de la peinture impressionniste' | S39 | • La valeur relative des peintres<br>• Les oeuvres impressionnistes les plus importantes | • Négocier, persuader (S4)<br>• Travailler en groupe (écouter, participer, encourager les autres) (S3,S4) |
| 9 Test de fin de thème | W45 | | • Planifier et écrire une rédaction selon les critères fournis (W2,W3) |

### 10 Activités de soutien

1 Visite au musée d'Orsay pendant l'échange.
2 Visite à l'exposition 'Monet in the 90s' à la Royal Academy
3 Exposition d'affiches artistiques appartenant au lycée.

### 11 L'Assistant(e)

1 Comment décrire les tableaux.
Sélection apportée par le groupe.
2 Comment comparer des tableaux. Sélection apportée par le groupe.
3 Débat: 'Les Tournesols' coûtent top cher!

*Choice and placing of material*

Since it is important not to overload the students with material, only three texts have been selected, presenting a contrast in format and register. The first is of the kind one might find in an art history, the second comes from an exhibition catalogue and the third is a newspaper article about recent thefts in the art world. It is very easy to keep presenting written material of the same kind. It is quite difficult to vary and balance the register, but essential if the students are not to become narrow in linguistic experience or bored by the monotony of the presentation.

Interspersed with the texts are oral activities of a substantial nature (discussion/presentation) and two sections of listening material, each with a transcript of the tape. Often, classes have access to listening facilities at specified times of the week and so the timing of these pieces needs to be planned accordingly. The 'set piece' oral activities are strategically placed; the initial discussion can only go at the beginning, the *'présentations individuelles'* (p 148) have to be situated well into the topic, firstly to give students preparation time (if it is to be a major item then several days if not a week of class time might be devoted to research, planning and preparation) and secondly so that they already have a good grasp of the vocabulary and lexis before embarking on the research; the *'exposition'* discussion (p 151) can only be done near the end of the topic, and after the presentations, so that students are well enough informed to make the necessary judgments.

*Activités de soutien/use of assistant*

If one is lucky enough to have the use of an assistant, it makes sense to integrate the work done by the assistant into the topic currently being studied. Sometimes, the assistant will have some good ideas about how to deal with the topic. Often she/he will need help and direction. The items at the foot of the summary sheet are suggestions for three different activities which could be undertaken without duplicating class work. They can therefore be done as and when appropriate.

This topic has some obvious follow-up work which can be undertaken out of class, though that may not be so with all topics. Whenever possible, we should seek to link students' work with the 'real world'. In the case of art, it is important to take them to look at paintings. 1990 was a good year, coinciding with the Monet exhibition in London. If students go on exchange, they may be able to visit the Musée d'Orsay in Paris and see many of the originals of pictures they have seen illustrated. At the very least, it must be possible for them to go to a local art gallery.

# 1 TRAVAIL ORAL PREPARATOIRE

**Peut-être que vous vous intéressez déjà à la peinture ou peut-être que vous ne commencez qu'à la découvrir. Répondez aux questions suivantes, en donnant autant de détails que possible dans vos réponses.**

**Voici quelques expressions pour vous aider:**

- j'aime beaucoup ...
- j'aime surtout ...
- je n'apprécie pas tellement ...
- je suis très attiré(e) par ...
- l'oeuvre de ........ me passionne
- les tableaux de ......... me touchent beaucoup
- ce qui m'intéresse/m'attire/me captive/me séduit/me fascine chez ........ c'est ...
- j'ai entendu parler de ...
- je connais un peu l'oeuvre de ...

**(a) Est-ce que vous aimez regarder les tableaux?**

**(b) Vous est-il arrivé récemment de visiter une exposition?**

**(c) Quel genre de peinture préférez-vous?**

**(d) Préférez-vous les paysages, les portraits, les natures mortes ...?**

**(e) Faites-vous vous-même de la peinture, ou des dessins?**

**(f) Combien de peintres français pouvez-vous nommer?**

**(g) Connaissez-vous déjà quelques peintres impressionnistes?**

**(h) Pouvez-vous nommer quelques tableaux impressionnistes?**

*As a general principle, discussion about totally unprepared topics is not likely to be very productive. However, a brief exploration of issues in a relatively superficial way can help to 'break the ice'. For one thing, it may help to introduce a few key words, or on the other hand one might unsuspectingly discover hidden depths of knowledge/talent/interest. A key feature of this exercise is that some useful phrases are given beforehand (these can be added to at this stage or later). The discussion could be consolidated by repeating the activity in pairs. This could be followed by the projection of a selection of slides without commentary, to engage students' interest with the reality of looking at paintings after what may have been a rather tentative opening discussion. During this the students could note down anything which comes to mind (themes, atmosphere, etc).*

# 2 L'IMPRESSIONNISME

La peinture qu'un chroniqueur du *Charivari* qualifiait d'impressionniste en 1874 existait depuis quelque temps déjà quand elle fut baptisée. Le tableau même qui inspira cette appellation, ce fameux port du Havre que Monet avait intitulé *Impression, soleil levant* date de 1872. Et l'origine de la peinture impressionniste remonte au milieu des années soixante. Monet à ce moment-là travaille à Paris, dans la forêt de Fontainebleau ou sur les plages normandes. Il a ecouté les conseils de Boudin et de Jongkind, il médite les exemples de Courbet, de Corot, des peintres de Barbizon. A ses côtés Renoir, Pissarro, Sisley, Bazille, ses amis, ont à peu près les mêmes admirations que lui et ils avancent dans la même direction.

Après le scandale de l'*Olympia*, tous ces artistes se groupent autour de Manet, mais ils sont plus enclins à approuver l'attitude qu'il adopte à l'égard de la peinture officielle qu'à prendre exemple sur son style. Monet le montre bien lorsqu'en 1866-1867 il peint ses *Femmes au jardin*. D'abord, il les peint entièrement en plein air, ce qui est déjà une innovation. Ensuite, il indique les ombres dans les visages et les vêtements clairs non plus par des tons foncés mais par des teintes froides, des verts, des bleus, suscitant ainsi un jeu de couleurs qui est indépendant de la forme des objets, qui tend même à la disloquer. Certes, la dislocation y est seulement annoncée et les voiles atmosphériques y sont à peine perceptibles; l'artiste ne se départ pas encore d'un dessin dont la netteté appartient à la tradition de la peinture d'atelier plutôt qu'au plein air. Aussi la nouvelle manière s'affirme-t-elle avec plus de décision dans les paysages que Monet et Renoir vont peindre en 1869 à la fameuse baignade de *La Grenouillère*: les figures y étant vues à distance, ils peuvent concentrer leur attention sur le rôle de la lumière et de l'atmosphère qui seront les principaux héros de la peinture impressionniste. Le séjour que Monet et Pissarro feront à Londres pendant la guerre de 1870 hâtera l'évolution. A Londres les deux artistes voient en effet des Constable et des Turner et, s'ils ne les admirent pas sans réserve, ils trouvent néanmoins en eux des affinités et des encouragements.

La première exposition qui en 1874 réunit, das les ateliers du photographe Nadar à Paris, les promoteurs de la nouvelle peinture, est pour l'histoire de l'art en événement si mémorable que l'on incline à penser que ses organisateurs aussi ont dû en mesurer la portée et la souligner aux yeux du public. Il n'en est rien. Les artistes qui prennent part à cette manifestation se présentent aux Parisiens simplement sous le titre de *Société anonyme coopérative d'artistes peintres, sculpteurs, graveurs*, etc... . Ils ne songent pas à se réclamer d'un programme. Ils ne veulent pas constituer une école. Au reste, ils n'appartiennent pas tous à la même tendance et ils n'offrent pas tous les mêmes qualités. Ils sont trente à exposer, et huit d'entre eux seulement - Monet, Renoir, Pissarro, Sisley, Berthe Morisot, Guillaumin, Degas, Cézanne - deviendront célèbres sous le nom d'Impressionnistes (Bazille n'est plus parmi eux: il a été tué au cours de la guerre de 1870).

Est-ce à dire que ceux-là forment un groupe homogène? Leurs tempéraments sont divers et leurs préoccupations, nous le verrons, sur certains points opposées. Mais ils ont en commun le refus de toute ce qui est cher à la peinture officielle: les sujets historiques, mythologiques, sentimentaux, la facture « léchée », le coloris terne, bitumeux. Ils ont en commun aussi la résolution de faire une peinture actuelle: ils empruntent leurs sujets à la réalité ordinaire de leur époque et ils entendent exprimer leurs sensations avec sincérité, fussent-ils obligés pour cela d'enfreindre ou de rejeter les règles d'un tradition séculaire. Jusqu'à un certain degré, tous sont également d'accord pour fixer sur leur toile, non ce que l'ont sait des choses, mais uniquement ce que l'on aperçoit à l'instant précis où l'on peint. D'ailleurs, la plupart d'entre eux ont une prédilection pour les paysages vaporeux de l'Ile-de France, pour les ciels que des nuages ne cessent de métamorphoser, pour le scintillement des reflets sur les eaux mouvantes de la Seine ou de l'Oise.

L'analyse des phénomènes lumineux les conduit à innover aussi dans le domaine de la technique: ils ne mettent plus sur leurs palettes que les couleurs du prisme et ils tiennent compte de la loi des complémentaires. Sachant que deux complémentaires que l'on met côte à côte s'exaltent, alors qu'elles se détruisent mutuellement si on les mélange, ils posent leurs couleurs pures en petites taches, en virgules, sans éviter toujours, il est vrai, que celles-ci se croisent ou s'enchevêtrent. Car leurs principes, ils les appliquent d'instinct et non de façon systématique. Néanmoins leur peinture devient beaucoup plus claire que celle de tous leurs devanciers depuis Léonard de Vinci, et le monde extérieur y possède un fraîcheur, un jeunesse, une diversité de la lumière surtout que l'on n'avait encore jamais connues dans l'art européen.

**L'Olympia:** un tableau de Manet (1863) qui suscita au Salon de 1865 un scandale sans précédent

**La Grenouillère:** un établissement situé sur la Seine, à Croissy, entre Chatou et Bougival, où les Parisiens allaient pour s'amuser

## Exercice 1

**Trouvez dans la liste à droite la définition qui correspond au mot à gauche.**

| MOTS | DEFINITIONS |
|---|---|
| 1 l'ombre | A causer, provoquer |
| 2 un ton foncé | B qui reflète mal la lumière |
| 3 susciter | C la salle où travaille le peintre |
| 4 une voile | D quelqu'un qui précède/a précédé |
| 5 un atelier | E un tableau représentant la nature |
| 6 homogène | F zone sombre créée par un object interceptant les rayons du soleil |
| 7 terne | G devenir mélangé |
| 8 un paysage | H qui possède une unité |
| 9 la portée | I une couleur sombre |
| 10 scintillement | J l'effet/l'importance |
| 11 se croiser | K ce qui cache quelque chose (p.ex. le visage) |
| 12 un devancier | L une lumière vibrante et intermittente |

| 1 | 2 | 3 | 4 | 5 | 6 | 7 | 8 | 9 | 10 | 11 | 12 |
|---|---|---|---|---|---|---|---|---|---|---|---|
| | | | | | | | | | | | |

## Exercice 2

**Ce texte contient de nombreux exemples de mots qui sont étroitement liés en forme et en sens à des mots anglais. Traduisez en anglais les mots soulignés:**

(a) quand elle fut baptisée ____________________

(b) il médite les exemples de Courbet ____________________

(c) ils sont plus enclins à approuver ____________________

(d) des tons foncés ____________________

(e) des teintes froides ____________________

(f) le séjour hâtera l'évolution ____________________

(g) ils ne veulent pas constituer une école ____________________

## Exercice 3

**Choisissez parmi les paires de sous-titres suivants celui qui résume le mieux chacun des 5 paragraphes du texte.**

| | | | |
|---|---|---|---|
| Paragraphe | 1 | A | 'Fontainebleau: vrai berceau de l'Impressionnisme' |
| | | B | 'Monet et les débuts' |
| Paragraphe | 2 | A | 'Naissance d'un nouveau style' |
| | | B | 'Peintres qui ont influencé les impressionnistes' |
| Paragraphe | 3 | A | 'Une exposition indépendante' |
| | | B | 'Rien en commun' |
| Paragraphe | 4 | A | 'L'unité des huit' |
| | | B | 'Des sujets peu permanents' |
| Paragraphe | 5 | A | 'Rôle central de la lumière' |
| | | B | 'Couleurs pures et distinctes' |

## Exercice 4

*Travail oral et écrit à deux*

**Selon les détails donnés dans le texte, expliquez la signifiance des noms/titres suivants pour l'histoire de l'Impressionnisme. Utilisez vos propres termes là où vous pouvez.**

| NOM/TITRE | SIGNIFIANCE POUR L'IMPRESSIONNISME |
|---|---|
| 1 'Impression, soleil levant' de Monet | |
| 2 Boudin, Jongkind | |
| 3 Renoir, Pissarro, Sisley, Bazille | |
| 4 Manet | |
| 5 'Femmes au Jardin' de Monet | |
| 6 La Grenouillère | |
| 7 Londres | |
| 8 L'Ile de France | |

## Exercice 5

**Remplissez les cases ci-dessous avec les détails convenables. Le premier exemple a déjà été fait pour vous montrer comment.**

| VERBE | SUJET | TEMPS | INFINITIF |
|---|---|---|---|
| qualifiait<br>inspira<br>peint<br>est annoncée<br>seront<br>ont dû<br>appartiennent<br>aperçoit<br>sachant | **un chroniqueur** | **imparfait** | **qualifier** |

## Exercice 6

**Remplissez les cases ci-dessous avec un mot convenable (à l'aide d'un dictionnaire, si besoin est)**

| VERBE | SUBSTANTIF |
|---|---|
| qualifier | **la qualification** |
| travailler | |
| avancer | |
| | la direction |
| annoncer | |
| | une évolution |
| | un photographe |
| | un promoteur |
| mesurer | |
| | la résolution |
| rejeter | |

## Exercice 7

*Travail oral et écrit à deux*

**Exprimez les phrases ci-dessous d'une façon différente, mais en gardant toujours le même sens.**

p.ex.'il médite les exemples de Courbet'
**il regarde et réfléchit sur les tableaux de Courbet**

(a) 'ont à peu près les mêmes admirations que lui'

___

(b) 'Après le scandale de l'Olympia'

___

(c) '(les voiles atmosphériques) y sont à peine perceptibles'

___

(d) 'Ils empruntent leurs sujets à la réalité ordinaire de leur époque'

___

(e) 'ont une prédilection pour les paysages vaporeux'

___

## Exercice 8

*Travail oral à deux, après présentation pour les devoirs*

**A tour de rôle, et sans regarder le texte ni utiliser des notes, donnez autant de détails que possible sur les aspects suivants. Utilisez vos propres termes si c'est commode.**

A les origines de la peinture impressionniste
B Monet/Renoir et les tableaux faits en plein air
A La première exposition 'impressionniste'
B Ce que les artistes ont en commun
A Les impressionnistes et les couleurs

## Exercice 9

*Travail écrit*

**Imaginez que vous étiez parisien(ne) au moment de l'exposition, et que vous venez de la visiter. Un(e) ami(e) de province va prochainement passer quelques jours à Paris. Ecrivez-lui une lettre brève pour décrire vos réactions à l'exposition et pour lui persuader d'y aller/de ne pas perdre son temps. (150 mots)**

*For purposes of illustration, a generous number of exercises have been devised (9). Not every passage will lead to such full exploitation, though as a rule it is more effective to study few texts in depth rather than numerous texts sketchily. The first two exercises help prepare the student for the text (**Exercise 1** can be done before reading) by concentrating on elements of vocabulary. **Exercise 2** reminds them, when tackling a new topic, that meaning can often be guessed through existing knowledge. **Exercises 3 and 4** help develop comprehension, the former in general terms (this one might be best done in pairs or threes and could lead to some interesting debate) and the latter more specifically, focusing on important information in the text. The function of **Exercises 5 to 7** is to consolidate and extend linguistic knowledge, though the more difficult **Exercise 7** lends itself well to pairwork and inevitably involves appraisal, discussion of content. Most of **Exercises 1-7** can and should be done for homework, though 3 and 7 need class contact. Only after such acquaintance with the text and its language can students hope to tackle **Exercise 8**, which will need feedback and class discussion to maximise its effect. Extended writing naturally occurs at the end of the suite of exercises. **Exercise 9** should be looked upon as a 'fun' piece, and, given its nature, should be written in a limited time.*

# 3 QUELQUES INFLUENCES SUR LA PEINTURE IMPRESSIONNISTE

ENREGISTREMENT

A: Alors dans l'impressionnisme on a déjà rencontré Monet. Quels autres noms faut-il retenir?

B: Pissarro, Renoir, Sisley, Degas, Cézanne, Berthe Morisot et d'autres moins connus, parfois injustement, comme Caillebotte, par exemple, et l'Américaine Mary Cassatt. Et il faut inclure Manet, bien qu'il ait toujours refusé de participer aux expositions du groupe. D'ailleurs, pendant les premières années, les adversaires des impressionnistes les appelaient 'la bande à Manet'. D'autres, comme Gauguin, débuteront par l'impressionnisme, pour ensuite orienter la peinture dans d'autres directions, le symbolisme, le fauvisme, mais ça, c'est une autre histoire, n'est-ce-pas?

A: L'impressionnisme n'a pas dû arriver du jour au lendemain. Qu'est-ce qui a donc préparé le terrain?

B: Là, il faut revenir sur la peinture de paysage en France avant les impressionnistes. Le paysage tel que l'envisageait l'Ecole des Beaux-Arts, était un paysage purement imaginaire, idéalisé. Le paysage académique ne s'intéressait pas du tout aux effets réels de la lumière naturelle. En général il servait de décor à un événement historique ou mythologique. Sa lumière était artificielle, plutôt théâtrale disons. C'est surtout Corot et les paysagistes de l'Ecole de Barbizon - Ecole de Barbizon parce qu'ils peignaient à Barbizon, petit village dans la forêt de Fontainebleau - ce sont surtout ces peintres qui ont amené la peinture de paysage vers plus de vérité.

A: De quelle façon?

B: Corot, par exemple, pour reproduire sur la toile les effets de la lumière naturelle, ajoutait du blanc à ses teintes. Comme ça elles conservaient plus de luminosité. Souvent il peignait le paysage à une certaine distance pour qu'on ne voie pas trop les détails et qu'on saisisse mieux l'harmonie générale. Corot disait qu'il ne fallait - je cite "jamais perdre la première impression qui nous a émus". Ce sera la devise des impressionnistes.

A: Et pourtant il y a un monde entre Corot et les impressionnistes.

B: C'est sûr. Et ce monde, c'est le romantisme. Les paysages de Corot et de l'Ecole de Barbizon montrent des idées romantiques sur la nature, lieu de calme, de solitude où on échappait à la ville, où on retrouvait les rythmes naturels des saisons. Cette nature-là n'intéresse pas beaucoup les impressionnistes sauf Pissarro peut-être.

A: C'est-à-dire, entre Corot et les impressionnistes, il y a Courbet, Manet, Baudelaire.

B: Oui, il y a le réalisme de Courbet, pour qui la réalité sociale contemporaine est le vrai sujet de la peinture. Il y a le modernisme de Manet, ses sujets scandaleux comme Olympia en 1865, cette femme nue, sensationnelle, non pas parce qu'elle est nue - des femmes nues il y en avait partout dans la peinture de l'Ecole des Beaux-Arts - mais parce qu'elle est moderne. Ce n'est pas une nymphe telle que Bouguereau les aimait, ce n'est pas une déesse. C'est une jeune femme moderne plus ou moins prostituée et son regard direct, franc s'adresse au spectateur. Là, Manet y est allé très fort. Sans parler des audaces techniques, cet emploi de couleurs claires et foncées posées à plat, sans modelé, aussi scandaleux que le sujet. Et du grand ami de Manet, le poète Baudelaire, il y avait les idées sur le peintre de la vie moderne.

A: Pourtant il ne faudra pas laisser croire que l'impressionnisme n'a eu que des sources exclusivement françaises. Il y avait des influences étrangères, les estampes japonaises notamment.

B: Il est certain que les estampes jamponaises ont été très importantes parce qu'elles ne se servaient ni de la perspective, ni du modelé, tels qu'on les pratiquait dans la tradition française, occidentale, depuis le quinzième siècle. A la place du modelé, du relief, elles montraient des couleurs vives posées côte à côte. A la place de la perspective, il y avait cet aspect plat si caratéristique de l'art japonais. L'Ecole des Beaux-Arts prétendait que la tradition académique occidentale était la seule valable, la forme la plus élevée de l'expression artistique, et voilà que l'art japonais démontrait le contraire, qu'il était possible de représenter la nature autrement.

A: On a beaucoup parlé aussi de l'importance de la photographie pour les impressionnistes.

B: A partir de la découverte de la photographie, vouloir donner une image objective du monde n'avait plus de sens pour un peintre. L'appareil photo le faisait mieux, plus facilement, plus rapidement. Il s'agissait donc d'interpréter le monde, et pour le peintre impressionniste, ça voulait dire, traduire sa perception personnelle, subjective de la réalité telle que la lumière la créait pour lui. Et plus, les premiers appareils photo n'étaient pas très sophistiqués. Ils ne reproduisaient pas toutes ces graduations entre la lumière et l'ombre que l'Ecole des Beaux-Arts aimait tellement. Ils habituaient les gens à des images plus naturelles, plus spontanées du monde.

## Exercice 1

**Avant d'écouter l'enregistrement, trouvez dans la liste à droite la phrase ou l'expression qui correspond à chacune des phrases à gauche.**

| PHRASES DE L'ENREGISTREMENT | EXPLICATION/DEFINITION |
|---|---|
| 1 il faut aussi inclure | A prendre une direction différente |
| 2 qui vont débuter | B ce qui nous a touchés tout d'abord |
| 3 s'orienter vers une autre forme | C l'idée centrale des impressionnistes |
| 4 du jour au lendemain | D qui commenceront |
| 5 ils servent de décor | E des techniques de peinture choquantes |
| 6 la première impression qui nous ait émus | F ils étaient comme des scènes théâtrales |
| 7 la devise des impressionnistes | G c'est nécessaire d'incorporer |
| 8 une nymphe | H une sorte de déesse |
| 9 des audaces techniques | I soudain, d'un jour à l'autre |

| 1 | 2 | 3 | 4 | 5 | 6 | 7 | 8 |
|---|---|---|---|---|---|---|---|
| | | | | | | | |

## Exercice 2

*jusqu'à '... les idées sur la peinture de la vie moderne'*

**Remplissez les cases ci-dessous avec les détails nécessaires.**

| | |
|---|---|
| les noms des principaux impressionnistes | |
| le titre donné par leurs adversaires | |
| le genre de paysage envisagé par l'Ecole des Beaux-Arts | |
| le rôle du paysage dans la peinture académique | |
| l'importance/la qualité de la lumière dans les tableaux académiques | |
| les artistes qui ont changé le rôle du paysage | |
| les différences qu'ils ont amenées | |
| le facteur commun entre Corot et les impressionnistes | |

## Exercice 3

*'Pourtant, il ne faudrait pas laisser croire ... des images plus naturelles, plus spontanées du monde'*

**Complétez les phrases suivantes. Attention, il ne faut pas toujours copier exactement!**

(a) Les sources de l'impressionnisme étaient ______________________________

______________________________

(b) Les estampes japonaises avaient ______________________________

______________________________

(c) A la place du relief, on ______________________________

______________________________

(d) L'art japonais démontrait que ______________________________

______________________________

(e) Après la découverte de la photographie, les peintres ne voulaient ______________

______________________________

(f) C'est plus facile pour l'appareil-photo

______________________________

## Exercice 4

*Travail oral à deux (10 minutes)*

**Après l'écoute de l'enregistrement, mettez vos idées en commun avec votre partenaire sur les aspects suivants.**

(a) les différentes attitudes envers le paysage
(b) l'influence des estampes japonaises
(c) l'influence de la photographie

## Exercice 5

*Travail oral en groupes de 3 ou 4*

**Après l'écoute de l'enregistrement, considérez chacune des questions suivantes. Le professeur vous donnera une période limitée pour arriver à chaque décision. Si vous vous trouvez d'accord dès le début, examinez toutes vos raisons et développez-les.**

(a) Préférez-vous regarder un tableau classique du modelé (relief) ou un tableau 'plat' (comme ceux de Gauguin)? (Votre professeur vous montrera des exemples des deux)

(b) Préférez-vous regarder une belle photographe ou un beau tableau?

*Students often have difficulty picking out individual words in a recording. For this reason, the preparatory exercise (**Exercise 1**) picks out a number of phrases which might cause them problems, but puts the onus on them to work out the meaning by selecting from a list. **Exercises 2 and 3** (one comprehension exercise on each section of the tape) pinpoint useful information which, after consolidation through correction, should serve as the basis for the productive **Exercise 4**. (The importance of using listening as a stimulus to other activities has already been mentioned in Chapter 3.) Clearly, Exercise 4 needs to be done as soon as possible after 2 and 3. However, the length of these might demand an hour or so alone; if Exercise 4 has to be separated, it might be preceded by a single replay of the tape as a 'refresher' or, if students can take copies of the tape home, it can be done at the next class meeting. **Exercise 5** allows a broadening of the discussion, using some of the notions in the tape as a springboard for students to air their own opinions and think for themselves. The tape will have given them enough 'technical' vocabulary to cope.*

# 4 QUAND TE MARIES-TU?

**[Pour ces exercices, il est essentiel que les étudiants puissent voir une illustration (en couleurs) de ce tableau de Gauguin.]**

## Nafea Faaipoipo (Quand te maries-tu?)

*Nafea Faaipoipo (Quand te maries-tu ?)*[1] est avant tout une composition décorative qui joue sur les rappels et oppositions de couleurs complémentaires, et dont l'atmosphère évoque le mystère de l'adolescence. On l'a souvent rapprochée d'une lettre de Gauguin à sa femme, écrite sans doute vers la fin avril 1892, où il expliquait : « Je suis en plein travail, maintenant je connais le sol, son odeur et les Tahitiens que je fais d'une façon très énigmatique n'en sont pas moins des Maoris et non des Orientaux des Batignolles. »[2] Pour la question de la date de ce tableau, il ne faut peut-être pas négliger la comparaison avec *Aha oe feii?* (cat. 153), à la palette relativement restreinte, et *Où vas-tu ?* (W 458 et W 501), toiles exécutées dans la seconde moitié de l'année. De fait, un petit croquis des personnages de *Nafea Faaipoipo* se trouve au dos d'une feuille d'études pour *Aha oe feii ?*[3].

Gauguin devait être obsédé par le personnage accroupi et bien décidé à l'utiliser dans une composition, car on le retrouve dans de petites esquisses préparatoires pour des peintures qui n'ont pas vu le jour[4]. L'artiste a également introduit ce personnage dans une petite esquisse à l'huile (W 455), et il l'a encore représenté sur une feuille de carnet, dans deux aquarelles[5] et dans un dessin préparatoire en grandeur réelle (cat. 146).

Field propose un précédent japonais[6] pour ce personnage, mais il semblerait que Gauguin ait pris pour point de départ la femme située à l'extrême droite dans les *Femmes d'Alger* de Delacroix (Musée du Louvre)[7]. Cette allusion aurait une signification évidente, étant donné l'immense admiration de Gauguin pour Delacroix, dont témoigne indéniablement le parallèle entre le pèlerinage artistique de Delacroix en Afrique du Nord, en 1832, et celui de Gauguin à Tahiti, presque soixante ans après. Gauguin avait une prédilection pour le personnage accroupi de *Nafea Faaipoipo*, qui revient dans trois autres tableaux de la première période tahitienne (W 447, W 478 et W 501). Même la forme de la pierre (portant la signature de l'artiste) au premier plan paraît répondre au mouvement sinueux massif des jambes et des hanches de ce personnage.

Dans leurs analyses de cette peinture, à peu près tous les spécialistes ont attiré l'attention sur le titre choisi par Gauguin, qu'il faut peut-être rapprocher de sa longue description du mariage tahitien dans *Noa Noa*, ou même du roman à succès où Loti a conté l'idylle d'un Européen et d'une Tahitienne, *Le Mariage de Loti* (1879). Cependant, il est impossible de savoir qui pose la question « Quand te maries-tu ? »[7] Field suppose que la fleur portée par la femme du premier plan indique qu'elle cherche un mari, et il interprète le second personnage comme son alter ego[8]. Pour lui, le geste de ce deuxième personnage serait inspiré de l'art bouddhique. Naomi Maurer voit dans ce geste un *mudra* bouddhique, signifiant l'enseignement, et elle pense que les deux personnages représentent deux étapes de la sensibilisation à l'expérience universelle de l'amour[9].

Alors même que Teha'amana a peut-être posé pour les deux personnages, il semble évident que Gauguin voulait opposer ces deux femmes placées l'une devant l'autre, la première tournant le dos à la seconde. Leurs regards sont orientés dans deux directions contraires et leurs vêtements sont différents. La première porte un paréo rouge vif (et non mauve pâle comme dans le dessin préparatoire), tandis que sa compagne est vêtue d'une robe de mission d'un rose corail très doux. Ces tons soigneusement orchestrés semblent désigner deux tempéraments distincts, au même titre que les poses différentes. Ainsi réunies, les deux protagonistes pourraient avoir un rapport avec les deux autres personnages minuscules debout dans le fond. Mais on ne sait s'il faut donner un sens à ce détail, ou au paysage et à sa mare limpide. Les deux branches feuillues qui pendent dans l'angle supérieur gauche de la composition, tels des accents décoratifs, sont peut-être à interpréter comme un faire-valoir métamorphique pour l'arbre apparemment mort dont les deux troncs se dressent à un bout de la mare.

Gauguin confia six peintures, dont celle-ci, au marchand Durand-Ruel après son exposition personnelle de novembre 1893. C'était l'une des deux œuvres pour lesquelles il demandait le prix le plus élevé, 1 500 F, preuve de l'importance qu'il lui accordait[10]. C.F.S.

*Nafea Faaipoipo* by Gauguin reproduced by kind permission of Réunion des Musées Nationaux

## Exercice 1

**Cherchez le sens des mots suivants dans un dictionnaire, et soyez prêt(e) à les expliquer en classe.**

- une palette
- une toile
- un croquis
- accroupi
- une esquisse
- une aquarelle
- un pèlerinage
- une étape
- une mare
- confier

## Exercice 2

**Lesquels des éléments suivants d'une analyse ont été utilisés par l'auteur dans son commentaire sur le tableau? Cochez ceux que vous pouvez trouver, et mettez la lettre qui correspond à côté du bon endroit dans le texte. (Ils suivent l'ordre du texte.)**

A une référence à l'ambiance créée par le tableau
B une citation de quelque chose écrite par l'artiste lui-même
C une référence à la tranquillité de la scène
D une citation de quelque chose écrite par un historien d'art
E une comparaison entre les couleurs de ce tableau et celles d'un autre tableau de Gauguin
F une référence à la signifiance des gestes des personnages
G un effort pour le dater
H une référence à des dessins préparatoires
I une référence au rôle de Tahiti dans l'art de Gauguin
J une conclusion personnelle tirée par l'auteur concernant l'origine des personnages
K une référence à la valeur décorative du tableau
L une analyse des théories différentes
M une comparaison entre le style de Gauguin et celui d'un autre peintre
N un commentaire au sujet du rapport entre les deux femmes
O un effort pour interpréter le rôle du paysage dans le tableau
P une référence à la destination de ce tableau

## Exercice 3

*Travail écrit à deux*

**Avec votre partenaire, et travaillant aussi rapidement que possible, donnez les détails nécessaires concernant ce que l'on dit dans le texte sur ...**

| | DETAILS |
|---|---|
| la qualité décorative | |
| la date du tableau | |
| l'attitude de Gauguin envers le personnage accroupi | |
| les différentes versions de ce personnage | |
| les origines possibles de ce personnage | |
| l'interprétation du titre par Field | |
| l'interprétation du titre par N Maurer | |
| les différences entre les deux femmes du tableau | |

## Exercice 4

**Cherchez dans le texte tous les exemples que vous pouvez trouver de substantifs + adjectifs utilisés pour décrire le tableau. Classez-les de la manière suivante:**

| MASCULIN (SINGULIER) | FEMININIONS (SINGULIER) |
| --- | --- |
| p.ex. **le personnage accroupi** | |

| MASCULIN (PLURIEL) | FEMININ (PLURIEL) |
| --- | --- |
| | **deux directions contraires** |

## Exercice 5

*Travail oral à deux*

**(Avec un partenaire différent, et regardant seulement le tableau, pas le texte)**

**Posez des questions à votre partenaire, à tour de rôle, au sujet de ce tableau. Essayez de traiter des aspects qui se trouvent dans le texte.**

## Exercice 6

*Présentations orales individuelles devant un petit groupe*

**Choisissez un tableau par un peintre français, qui vous plaît et faites des recherches sur ce tableau et sur le peintre. Préparez une présentation orale de 3 minutes là-dessus (ne passez pas trop de temps à parler de la vie de l'artiste - seulement si c'est important pour la compréhension du tableau).**

**Vous devez décrire le tableau à la classe, et expliquer les <u>techniques</u> utilisées par l'artiste. N'oubliez pas de penser:**

- à l'artiste
- à la date du tableau
- à son ambiance/atmosphère
- à ses couleurs
- à sa construction
- au contenu
- au symbolisme (s'il y en a)
- au titre
- à des comparaisons avec d'autres tableaux

**Pour notes, vous pouvez utiliser seulement 45 mots!!**

*The main intention of this text is not specifically to inform about Gauguin, rather to sensitise students to paintings, begin to think about painters' techniques and interpret them visually, and understand that a relationship may exist between the painter's life and his work. The vocabulary work is tackled in a different way from earlier parts of this topic (**Exercise 1**), whilst ideas on techniques and the means of expressing them come into **Exercise 2**, which requires careful and detailed reading (time-consuming: best done for homework). After this laborious work, **Exercise 3** is designed to encourage speed-reading and will at the same time consolidate language. **Exercise 4** enables some revision of adjectival agreement - appropriate when students are learning how to describe. Some further re-reading of the text at home might help prepare students for the difficult **Exercise 5** (in effect an oral summary - they will need help with question forms), and **Exercise 6** is the natural culmination of work on the text. Since it asks students to perform 'devant un petit groupe', it builds up confidence for a major presentation later, though students should be guided against concentrating too much on the painter's life.*

## 5 LE CHOC DE L'IMPRESSIONNISME

ENREGISTREMENT

**A: Commençons par le début. Puisqu'il s'agit d'impressionnisme, d'où vient donc ce nom?**

**B: Eh bien pour pouvoir répondre, il faut d'abord expliquer qu'en France au milieu du 19e siècle, il n'y avait pas le système d'expositions dans des musées ou galeries que nous connaissons maintenant. Il n'y avait que le Salon, c'est-à-dire l'exposition annuelle organisée par l'Ecole des Beaux-Arts. Donc un peintre, pour pouvoir vendre ses toiles, devait obligatoirement les faire accepter par le Salon. Ce Salon avait un jury, composé pour la plupart de peintres conservateurs, en général des professeurs de l'Ecole des Beaux-Arts, et ce jury décidait quels tableaux étaient dignes d'être présentés au public dans l'exposition annuelle.**

**A: L'Ecole des Beaux-Arts exerçait donc un véritable monopole sur l'enseignement, l'exposition et la vente de la peinture en France.**

**B: C'est ça.**

**A: Alors, être refusé par le Salon, c'était grave pour un peintre.**

**B: Très grave. Le public achetait les tableaux qui avaient du succès au Salon. Alors, un groupe de jeunes peintres, qui avaient tous été refusés à plusieurs reprises par le jury, a décidé de former une association pour organiser des expositions indépendantes, hors du contrôle du Salon. La première a eu lieu en 1874. Un certain Claude Monet y a présenté une toile intitulée *Impression, soleil levant*, qu'il avait peinte en 1872. Un journaliste, Louis Leroy, s'en est servi pour appeler ces peintres les 'impressionnistes'.**

**A: Le mot était donc une forme d'insulte, d'injure.**

**A: C'est ça. Le journaliste imaginait une conversation entre lui-même et un Monsieur Vincent, peintre célèbre et décoré:**

- **Que représente cette toile?**
- **Impression, soleil levant.**
- **Impression, j'en étais sûr. Je me disais aussi, puisque je suis impressionné, il doit y avoir de l'impression, là-dedans ...**

**Quelques jours plus tard, un autre journaliste, qui s'appelait Castagnary et qui défendait Courbet et les réalistes, expliquait que Monet et les autres étaient des impressionnistes en ce sens qu'ils rendaient non le paysage, mais la sensation produite par le paysage. C'est l'impression personnelle qui domine et non plus la représentation objective d'un paysage.**

**A: Visiblement la distinction n'a pas été comprise en 1874. Mais pourquoi? Pourquoi ces tableaux ont-ils provoqué un scandale à l'époque?**

**B: Parce que l'impressionnisme représentait le refus de toute la tradition picturale enseignée par l'Ecole des Beaux-Arts. Prenons un exemple précis. Au Salon de 1873, un des tableaux les plus remarqués était celui d'un certain William Bouguereau, *Nymphes et satyre*. Rien que le titre, n'est-ce pas? Le tableau montre quatre belles jeunes filles, les nymphes, nues évidemment, qui cherchent à entraîner un satyre vers l'eau. Un satyre c'est un dieu mythologique qui a un corps humain, des cornes et des pieds de chèvre - mélange divin, humain et animal si vous voulez. Alors les nymphes cherchent à entraîner le**

satyre vers l'eau mais visiblement le satyre, lui, n'y tient pas. Dans le catalogue du Salon le tableau est accompagné de quelques vers en latin et leur traduction qui explique tout: 'Conscient de sa peau velue, et n'ayant pas appris à nager dans son enfance, il n'ose pas se plonger dans les eaux profondes'. Bon voilà, ce n'est qu'un exemple mais il est représentatif. Il faut savoir que Bouguereau était un des peintres les plus célèbres de l'époque. Ses tableaux coûtaient très cher. *Nymphes et satyre* a été vendu à un Américain pour 35.000 francs, une véritable fortune. Pour comparer, en 1878 Monet a reçu 210 francs pour *Impression, soleil levant*.

A: Ce qui veut dire qu'en 1874 pour l'Ecole des Beaux-Arts et donc pour le public aussi, forcément, la peinture c'était Bouguereau et non pas Monet. C'était *Nymphes et satyre* et non pas *Impression, soleil levant*.

B: C'est ça. Ces deux formes de peinture étaient contradictoires. Pour L'Ecole certains sujets étaient plus nobles que d'autres. Les plus nobles étaient ceux pris dans la mythologie grecque ou romaine, dans l'histoire de la religion ou dans l'histoire de France. Mais les impressionnistes peignaient La Seine à Bougival, les boulevards, les cafés, les ponts de chemin de fer. Ils voulaient être de leur époque, ils voulaient prendre leurs sujets dans la vie qui les entourait, des sujets que l'on trouvait dans les journaux illustrés plutôt que dans la peinture traditionnelle.

A: En plus de ces sujets nobles, l'Ecole des Beaux-Arts enseignait aussi une manière de peindre, toute une série de règles et de pratiques que l'étudiant devait apprendre.

B: Oui, et cet enseignement était très strict. L'étudiant apprenait d'abord à dessiner des formes (les sculptures antiques, le corps humain). Puis on apprenait le jeu de la lumière et de l'ombre sur ces formes, ce qu'on appelait le modelé parce que la transition entre la lumière et l'ombre modelait l'objet, lui donnait du relief, créait l'illusion de trois dimensions. Et quand on avait bien appris le dessin et le modelé, seulement à ce moment-là on apprenait à se servir de la couleur.

A: Et pourquoi cet ordre d'études?

B: Parce que pour l'Ecole des Beaux-Arts, la peinture, c'était d'abord le dessin. La couleur venait après parce que son rôle était subordonné à celui du dessin. La couleur devait mettre le dessin en valeur, elle devait souligner l'architecture du tableau. Le dessin, c'était le côté intellectuel de la peinture, la couleur le côté émotionnel et pour l'Ecole des Beaux-Arts, pour la tradition académique que l'Ecole représentait, l'esprit devait toujours dominer les émotions, les discipliner.

A: Comment donc les impressionnistes refuseront-ils ces règles?

B: Pour les impressionnistes la nature n'avait pas de lignes. Elle avait bien des couleurs mais pas de lignes. Donc ils éliminent les lignes, ils éliminent les contours abstraits. Pour les impressionnistes, le monde se présente à l'oeil en forme de taches de lumière colorée. Donc ils utilisent les couleurs et non pas des lignes pour construire, pour organiser leurs tableaux, pour créer le modelé, le relief. Et au lieu de mélanger ces couleurs sur leur palette, ce qui avait pour résultat de diminuer leur éclat, ils les posent pures sur la toile.

A: Et plus, ils montrent sur la surface du tableau les touches du pinceau.

B: Oui, parce que ce sont ces touches qui témoignent du travail du peintre, de son interprétation du sujet et donc de sa personnalité, son originalité. La tradition académique admettait que ces touches soient visibles sur les esquisses, les ébauches, les études que le peintre avait faites dans les premières phases de son tableau mais pas dans le version finale, définitive qui devait présenter une surface lisse, polie, d'où toute trace du pinceau avait été éliminée.

*Travail préparatoire*

**Le vocabulaire et les expressions ci-dessous vous seront expliqués avant l'écoute de l'enregistrement. Ceci vous donnera une idée de ce que vous allez entendre.**

**Vocabulaire et expressions**

des peintres conservateurs
des tableaux dignes d'être présentés au public
exercer un monopole
refusé(s) à plusieurs reprises par le jury
hors du contrôle
un journaliste s'en est servi
une injure
ils rendaient la sensation produite par le paysage
le refus
qui cherchent à entraîner un satyre vers l'eau
le satyre n'y tient pas
des vers en latin
les plus nobles étaient surpris dans la mythologie
la vie qui les entourait
une série de règles et de pratiques
le jeu de la lumière et de l'ombre
son rôle était subordonné à celui du dessin
mettre en valeur
l'esprit
une tâche
diminuer l'éclat des couleurs
les touches du pinceau
les esquisses et les ébauches
une surface lisse

**Noms propres**

L'Ecole des Beaux-Arts
Courbet et les Réalistes
William Bouguereau
Nymphes et satyres
La Seine à Bougival

## Exercice 1

**Ecoutez cet enregistrement et mettez les idées ci-dessous dans l'ordre où vous les entendez:**

1 l'origine du terme impressionniste
2 les différentes techniques entre les traditionalistes et les impressionnistes
3 la raison pour laquelle les tableaux impressionnistes ont causé un scandale
4 l'importance et l'influence du Salon
5 l'importance de la couleur pour les impressionnistes
6 une comparaison des sujets traditionnels et ceux des impressionnistes
7 l'exposition des artistes indépendants
8 une description de la peinture traditionnelle de l'époque

| 1 | 2 | 3 | 4 | 5 | 6 | 7 | 8 |
|---|---|---|---|---|---|---|---|
| | | | | | | | |

## Exercice 2

**Ecoutez de nouveau l'enregistrement et remplissez les cases avec les renseignements/ détails nécessaires.**

| | |
|---|---|
| 1 De quelle époque parle-t-on? | |
| 2 Quand le Salon avait-il lieu? | |
| 3 La composition du Jury | |
| 4 Le but du Jury | |
| 5 Les secteurs sur lesquels L'Ecole des Beaux-Arts exerçait un monopole | |
| 6 La date de la première exposition des Indépendants | |
| 7 Le titre du tableau célèbre que Monet a présenté | |
| 8 La définition du mot 'impressionniste', selon Castagniari | |
| 9 L'élément qui domine, pour lui | |
| 10 La raison pour laquelle ces tableaux ont provoqué un scandale | |
| 11 Le titre du tableau peint par Bouguereau | |
| 12 Le sujet de ce tableau | |
| 13 Qui était Bouguereau? | |
| 14 Le prix de son tableau | |
| 15 Le prix de 'Impression, soleil levant' | |
| 16 Les sujets les plus nobles (pour L'Ecole des Beaux-Arts) | |
| 17 Les sujets que peignaient les Impressionnistes | |
| 18 Où trouvaient-ils leurs sujets? | |
| 19 Qu'est-ce que les Impressionnistes éliminent? | |
| 20 L'effet de mélanger les couleurs | |
| 21 Qu'est-ce que les Impressionnistes montrent sur la surface du tableau? | |

## Exercice 3

*Travail oral à deux*

**Maintenant regardez de nouveau Exercice 1. A tour de rôle, faites un résumé oral à votre partenaire de chacune des huit sections mentionnées.**

*As with the earlier listening exercise (piece 3), some preparation of vocabulary is built in. Here words and phrases are highlighted. A shortcut to the class explanation of them might be homework preparation using dictionaries. Thus, words like 'une injure', 'le refus' could be explained by the students themselves. The purpose of such highlighting is merely to help students recognise sounds when they hear them - hence the need to write the proper names, though generally there is no need to include in a list of this kind words already met.* ***Exercise 1*** *is to develop gist comprehension, whilst* ***Exercise 2*** *is intentionally straightforward in its requirements. If time permits, further development can take place in the shape of* ***Exercise 3*** *(oral summary in pairs), which should be perfectly feasible after the detailed listening of Exercise 2.*

# 6 PRESENTATIONS INDIVIDUELLES

## Exercice 1

*Présentations orales individuelles*

**En travaillant seul(e) ou à deux, prenez un des peintres impressionnistes, ou bien un peintre qui a participé, pendant un certain temps, au groupe, et trouvez tout ce que vous pouvez à son sujet. Faites une sélection de ses tableaux et préparez un exposé pour la classe. Votre exposé devrait être spontané, à l'aide seulement, si besoin est, de quelques notes. Voici quelques indications pour vous aider, mais vous pouvez, bien sûr, changer l'ordre de ces éléments pour convenir à votre style personnel de présentation:**

quelques détails de sa vie

- date et lieu de naissance
- études
- influences
- lieux de travail

sa position par rapport aux impressionnistes

son importance

les thèmes de sa peinture

commentaires sur une sélection de ses oeuvres

- sujet
- composition
- technique
- atmosphère
- vos réactions personnelles

ce qui vous intéresse/ce qui vous plaît chez ce peintre

**Pendant les autres exposés, faites des notes selon les catégories citées et contribuez positivement à l'exposé en posant des questions ou en ajoutant vos propres opinions.**

*Detailed comments on the rationale behind student presentations can be found on p 91 (Developing speaking). When class size is big (say ten or more), the presentations can take a long time and lead to rather monotonous classes. Students who give their presentation early in the sequence may lose interest. See foot of p 91 for ways to avoid this.*

## 7 HARO SUR VAN GOGH ET CEZANNE

# Haro sur Van Gogh et Cézanne

***Trois tableaux prestigieux ont été volés au musée municipal d'Amsterdam. Un butin phénoménal, près de 300 millions de francs. Du jamais vu dans l'histoire des vols d'œuvres d'art.***

Le vol du siècle. Ce n'est pas cette fois une banque qui en a fait les frais mais le vénérable musée municipal d'Amsterdam où trois tableaux, un Van Gogh, un Cézanne et un Jongkind, ont été dérobés dans la nuit de jeudi à vendredi. Un trio fabuleux dont la valeur totale est estimée à

**PAR VALÉRIE DUPONCHELLE**

cent millions de florins, soit 52 millions de dollars, 296 millions de francs environ, et qui dépasse ainsi tout ce qui a été volé en matière d'œuvres d'art. De mémoire de collectionneur ou même de policier, on n'avait jamais vu ça. La disparition des Monet de Marmottan ou des Corot de Semur-en- Auxois fait à côté presque petite figure...

Avec la disparition de « Anjelieren » (Œillets) de Van Gogh (46 sur 37,5 cm), de « Bouteilles et pommes » (50 sur 52 cm), une nature morte de Cézanne peinte dans les années 1890-1894, et de « La Maison du maître Adam Billaud à Nevers » (56 sur 42 cm), peinte en 1874 par Jongkind, ce sont cent millions de florins et surtout un vrai trésor artistique qui se sont ainsi envolés du Stedelijk Museum d'Amsterdam. Une véritable *« catastrophe »*, selon le directeur du musée, M. W. Beeren, qui s'en est aussitôt pris à la *« négligence »* de la police, l'accusant de ne pas avoir réagi à l'alarme que les voleurs ont déclenchée en brisant une vitre du musée.

Cocktail de célébrités oblige, le vol d'Amsterdam bat tous les records enregistrés en matière de butin. Depuis le vol de « la Joconde » par l'Italien Vincenzo Peruggia en 1911, l'histoire de l'art est pourtant jonchée de ces vols spectaculaires et inestimables qui défraient la chronique par leur audace et leur technicité. Parce que les œuvres visées sont toujours uniques et donc irremplaçables, il est difficile de chiffrer avec exactitude le préjudice subi par les musées ou les collectionneurs. Reste que les estimations précédentes n'ont jamais atteint de pareilles sommes et que cette dernière affaire soulève déjà une émotion toute significative chez les connaisseurs de France et d'ailleurs.

### Difficile à écouler

*« Pensez ! C'est trente fois plus que les cinq Corot de Semur-en-Auxois... »*, souligne-t-on à l'Office central pour la répression des vols d'œuvres et objets d'art (OCRVOOA) qui s'est illustré en décembre dernier, en rapatriant du Japon quatre des cinq toiles volées en octobre 1984 dans le musée de la Côte-d'Or. Un retour au pays orchestré de main de maître par le commissaire Mireille Ballestrazzi, partie au pays du Soleil-Levant sur la piste de ces quatre tableaux estimés à un total de six millions de francs. Un retour qui marque l'aboutissement de trois ans d'enquête menée par les policiers français et qui traduit à elle seule l'ampleur de la tâche à accomplir pour faire la chasse à ces voleurs spécialisés et internationaux.

Jusqu'à présent, le record en valeur revenait au célébrissime *« Impression, soleil levant »* de Monet, qui donna son nom à l'impressionnisme. Volé en octobre 1985 au musée Marmottan, ce tableau mythique, toujours porté disparu, est estimé à 80 millions de francs. L'ensemble des neuf toiles volées au musée parisien cet automne-là, dont cinq Monet et deux Renoir, atteignait déjà la somme impressionnante de 100 à 200 millions de francs. L'arrestation, en avril dernier au Mexique, de Philippe Jamin, le voleur présumé des Corot de Semur-en-Auxois, et de ses complices, a redonné espoir de les voir resurgir un jour, peut-être prochain.

Le vol d'Amsterdam reste d'autant plus exceptionnel que les Pays-Bas sont peu souvent victimes de ce type de banditisme. Et ce, contrairement à la France et à l'Italie. Ainsi depuis 1954, 40 000 œuvres d'art auraient disparu en Italie et 12 000 en France, soit pour cette dernière une progression du trafic de 8 % par an. Près de 1 000 de nos musées de province sont particulièrement exposés, sans compter les églises et les édifices culturels. La menace est omniprésente. Le musée d'art et d'essai du Palais de Tokyo, le musée du Breuil de Langres, le musée Picasso d'Antibes, le musée de Bayonne, le musée de Bagnols-sur-Cèze ou le musée de Lyon ont tous reçu un jour la visite de ces voleurs de maîtres. Certains comme le musée des Beaux-Arts de Marseille ou le musée Fabre de Montpellier ont retrouvé leurs biens. Pas tous.

Environ 75 % des tableaux volés sont récupérés au bout de sept ans, car ils sont, heureusement, très difficiles à écouler. Ainsi les 14 tableaux, dont ceux de Monet, Boudin et Courbet, dérobés en janvier 1981 au musée de Morlaix (Finistère) et estimés à 10 millions de francs, ont été retrouvés après quatre ans de recherches, en juillet 1985. Parfois, comme dans le cas des 38 miniatures volées en juillet 1980 au musée Jacquemart-André de Paris, on n'en retrouve qu'une partie.. « Unique consolation, soupire cet enquêteur de l'office central, leur valeur n'attend pas le nombre des années ! »

**Valérie DUPONCHELLE.**

## Exercice 1

**Le reporter mentionne plusieurs vols de ces dernières années. Vous travaillez pour 'Interpol'! Complétez ce tableau, qui se trouve dans votre bureau, avec les détails qui manquent.**

| ANNEE DU VOL | PEINTRE(S) | TITRE/ NOMBRE DE TABLEAUX | MUSEE | VALEUR | RETROUVE(S)? CHANCES D'ETRE RETROUVE(S)? |
|---|---|---|---|---|---|
| | | 38 MINIATURES | | | |
| 1981 | | | | | |
| | COROT | | | | |
| | | | MUSEE MARMOTTAN | | |
| 1988 | | | | | |

## Exercice 2

*Travail oral*

**Discutez d'abord avec votre partenaire et ensuite avec les autres membres de la classe les questions suivantes:**

(a) Quelles sont les motivations possibles de ces vols de tableaux prestigieux?

(b) Est-ce qu'on peut contrôler la valeur financière des oeuvres d'art?

(c) Voudriez-vous posséder un tableau célèbre?

(d) Est-ce que les musées devraient mieux protéger leurs tableaux?

(e) Est-ce que le gouvernement devrait interdire les collections privées?

*This text and the accompanying exercises provide a refreshing contrast to what has gone before. The journalistic register provides linguistic variation, and the principal exercise helps develop the skill of scanning for specific information, reminding students that total knowledge of a text is not the only function of reading. Additionally, the text brings us into contact with an aspect of the topic with which students are likely to be acquainted - the enormity of the prices associated with impressionist pictures. If they have not already considered the tension between art and materialism, now is a good time for them to do so!*

# 8 EXPOSITION DE LA PEINTURE IMPRESSIONNISTE

## Exercice 1

*Travail oral de groupe (préparé individuellement)*

*(a) Travail individuel (10 minutes):*

**Vous travaillez dans un musée et on vous a demandé de choisir 10 tableaux impressionnistes pour une exposition représentant ce qu'il y a de mieux dans le mouvement impressionniste. Quels tableaux choisiriez-vous? Mettez-les en ordre de priorité.**

| PEINTRE | TABLEAU |
|---|---|
| 1 | |
| 2 | |
| 3 | |
| 4 | |
| 5 | |
| 6 | |
| 7 | |
| 8 | |
| 9 | |
| 10 | |

*(b) Travail de groupe à 3 ou à 4 (20-30 minutes):*

**Vous faites partie d'un comité qui décide sur le contenu de l'exposition. Mettez-vous d'accord sur les dix tableaux que vous allez exposer!**

*After the individual presentations, everyone will have an interest in seeing that 'their' painter is represented. In larger groups, there will be some keen debate selecting the painters! For this reason, it is as well not to allow more than eight or so to be represented. Students should be encouraged to justify carefully their selection both of artists and paintings. The individual preparation for this activity might be more effectively done for homework, so that students have time to remind themselves about different artists and the titles of paintings. To profit from the exercise, it is important that they do not collaborate.*

## 9 TEST DE FIN DE THEME

*Sujet de rédaction* (300-350 mots)

**Voici quelques sujets de rédaction sur ce thème. Vous devez en choisir un et le préparer à l'avance. Votre professeur vous demandera de l'écrire en classe, sans notes.**

1 **Vous êtes reporter pour une revue d'art internationale. Ecrivez le compte-rendu de la première exposition impressionniste.**

2 **Comparez les thèmes et les techniques de deux artistes impressionnistes. Lequel préférez-vous? Pourquoi?**

3 **Quels sont, pour vous, les attraits de l'art impressionniste? Utilisez des exemples précis pour illustrer vos opinions.**

*Nothing really needs to be added to the comments on essay-writing in Chapter 5 (Developing writing). However, it is worth remembering that students have, in this topic, already done a good deal of research and individual work on two oral presentations. So as not to overburden them, it would make sense in this context to limit the demands on their time. The best way to do this is to ask them to write the essay under controlled conditions (say 1½ hours of class time). As the topic is placed early in the second year, students' essay skills may still be relatively undeveloped: they should be given the title (or choice of titles) in advance, so that they can prepare them in a limited way, and the titles should be very closely related to the work they have covered - hence the brief selection here. If an important part of the objective of this topic is to be able to write an essay which will be marked according to certain criteria, it is essential to make these criteria available to students in advance and to give support in those areas where they may need it (e.g. planning, structure).*

## KEY POINTS

- A multi-skill approach reflects natural processes of language acquisition
- The structure of a given topic will depend on the content/language which needs to be covered and the resources available
- A summary sheet allows staff and students to see the specific objectives of the topic and lists the resources to be used
- It is helpful for students to know the order of work well in advance
- Topics should not be overlong: four to five weeks maximum
- The exercises and source materials selected are appropriate to the timing (early in fourth term)
- Textual material has been selected to give a balance
- There is gradual build-up of oral skills within the topic
- Listening pieces have been strategically placed, complementing reading and speaking
- The exercises based on texts tend to follow the graded approach, beginning with comprehension and leading through to productive exercises
- Listening can be a good stimulus for discussion
- There is variety in the exercise types used in the topic - none is repeated
- All the input (reading and listening exercises in particular) builds up towards the extended, productive exercises
- Demands on student time need to be balanced; lengthy oral presentations may be offset against a 'class' timed essay

## Chapter 7

# ASSESSMENT AND MONITORING

### The function of assessment

A programme of work cannot be coherent and effective unless the objectives are clearly defined and methods evolved by teachers to check that those objectives have been achieved. Such a scheme of assessment should take account of student performance throughout the course and is likely to be both formal and informal.

Assessment will sometimes entail a value judgment on the quality of a student's work, though it should aim to be as objective as possible if it is to be effective. In this context, assessment is something which is undertaken by the teacher (or student: see *Self-assessment* below) for internal purposes, although it can also, of course, be part of the examining process. The results of assessment should be recorded so that a clear overall picture of the student's work and progress can be obtained. This will inform future action by teacher and student.

### Assessing and recording

In the course of every module of work, students should be assessed on those aspects which have formed the main objectives of the module/unit/topic. The assessment may take the form of a prepared or an unprepared test, or it may be made on the basis of performance in one or more classroom activities.

The form will naturally depend on many factors, but it is important that students are only asked to achieve what it is possible for them to do. For example, there is no point in asking them to write a newspaper article about animal experiments if they have not been given any help on writing newspaper articles, however well they have covered the area of animal experiments. But if we can establish our objectives clearly, then it should not be too difficult to establish means of checking the extent to which those objectives have been reached.

Assessment should cover all the measurable objectives of the course, as defined in Chapters 1-5 above and should be properly recorded. It might, for example, feed into an individual Record of Progress, containing reference to all those objectives. Page 156 shows a sample record for the area of Writing. Where pieces of work are used to assess or test a student's progress in a specific category, a mark on the scale 1-4 is entered in the appropriate line. Some pieces of work (e.g. a piece of guided writing) may be used to test progress in a number of different categories listed under section 2, in which case marks would be entered in a number of different lines, including no 14, the global performance for Guided Writing. The marks 1-4 (headed poor to excellent for shorthand) are awarded against specific criteria for each skill (see *Performance criteria* below).

Additional pages of the Record need to be produced for Reading, Listening, Speaking, Language and Content. For Reading, the skills would relate directly to the five objectives listed on p 19, whilst for Listening and Speaking one would refer to the objectives on pages 57 and 74. Any of the objectives can be split into subsections (as for Writing) as appropriate.

Teachers may feel it unnecessary to produce a separate record for Language, since this is already covered by the skill areas. But the most difficult might be Content. Since the first-year topics are likely to be seen essentially as vehicles for developing the skills, albeit in the context of French culture, it may not be deemed necessary to define and assess knowledge of this kind. However, in the second year, where a body of knowledge is presumed, one ought logically to be able to define the general areas of knowledge within each topic. Thus it might be possible to produce a list of such areas thought to be fundamental to a given topic (e.g. 'Understand the area of animal experiments'). On the other hand, one could decide that this would be arbitrary, time-consuming and superficial - in which case a solution would be to omit content records entirely and assess it under Writing (see categories 6-10 on p 156).

Since assessment of this kind can be used in the course of routine pieces of work (e.g. a set of reading exercises), it need not produce any more work for the teacher than would be the case with routine marking and recording in a register. Obviously the range of 1-4 does not discriminate widely, but it is efficient enough in plotting general levels of achievement and trends in progress. The comprehensive and positive nature of keeping records like this links in well with Records of Achievement. Ideally, both student and teacher would need access to the records of work in French.

**FRENCH 'A' LEVEL RECORD OF PROGRESS** **AREA: WRITING**

NAME: .............................. COURSE/GROUP ..................

| | PERFORMANCE (1 = poor; 2 = average; 3 = good; 4 = excellent) | | | | | | | | | | | | | | |
|---|---|---|---|---|---|---|---|---|---|---|---|---|---|---|---|
| **SKILL** **ITEM NO.** | 1 | 2 | 3 | 4 | 5 | 6 | 7 | 8 | 9 | 10 | 11 | 12 | 13 | 14 | 15 |
| 1. Micro-writing | | | | | | | | | | | | | | | |
| 2. Fluency and naturalness | | | | | | | | | | | | | | | |
| 3. Accuracy | | | | | | | | | | | | | | | |
| 4. Variety of structures/syntax | | | | | | | | | | | | | | | |
| 5. Range of vocabulary | | | | | | | | | | | | | | | |
| 6. Task completion/relevance | | | | | | | | | | | | | | | |
| 7. Understanding topic/stimulus passage | | | | | | | | | | | | | | | |
| 8. Structure | | | | | | | | | | | | | | | |
| 9. Developing ideas | | | | | | | | | | | | | | | |
| 10. Detailed knowledge | | | | | | | | | | | | | | | |
| 11. Independence | | | | | | | | | | | | | | | |
| 12. Research skills | | | | | | | | | | | | | | | |
| 13. Presentation | | | | | | | | | | | | | | | |
| 14. Guided writing (global) | | | | | | | | | | | | | | | |
| 15. Discursive essay (global) | | | | | | | | | | | | | | | |

**Performance criteria**

Once a complete record has been produced containing references to all the skills defined, a set of 'performance criteria' can be formulated for every item in the list. On the following pages are some examples of criteria relating to objectives within the different areas of Writing, Speaking and Content. Sample A shows how marks would be awarded for category 4 on the Record of Progress (Writing) on p 156.

In formulating criteria by which to assess achievement of the objectives/skills tested, it might be helpful to bear the following points in mind:

- The full range (e.g. 1-4) should be used.
- The number of marks/grades available should always be the same, to allow students to compare their performance in one area against another.
- Criteria should be positive, to reflect what students can do.
- An even number of marks/grades is preferable, to counter the natural tendency to award marks in the middle of the range.
- A short scale of four or six bands is easier to write and to use, and gives sufficient differentiation.
- Any set of criteria should relate only to a single objective. Criteria relating to performance in two or more different areas (e.g. breadth of vocabulary, accuracy, fluency of language) cannot be defined adequately, as an individual's performance may easily differ in each area.

## PERFORMANCE CRITERIA: SAMPLE A

**Area**: Writing

**Skill 4**: Use a variety of linguistic structures, as appropriate

| | |
|---|---|
| 1 | Able to produce simple sentence patterns with few subordinate clauses. Contains anglicisms in sentence patterns or phrasing. |
| 2 | Able to vary sentence patterns, beginning occasionally with subordinate clauses, but linguistic/grammatical structures generally simple. |
| 3 | Uses more ambitious linguistic structures with an ability to vary sentence patterns well, but style rather heavy, stilted or anglicised. |
| 4 | Uses complex sentence patterns and structures with confidence. Includes rhetorical devices where appropriate. Reads easily. |

## PERFORMANCE CRITERIA: SAMPLE B

**Area**: Speaking

**Skill 4**: Negotiate/exchange information

| | |
|---|---|
| 1 | Can give information accurately and express basic point of view. |
| 2 | Understands opposing point of view/difficulties expressed by other party and can make some response. |
| 3 | Has a limited success in conveying point of view in the face of some opposition or successfully achieves straightforward objective. |
| 4 | Successfully achieves objective, despite problems or difficulties encountered, and displays politeness/tact as well as firmness. |

## PERFORMANCE CRITERIA: SAMPLE C

**Area**: Content

**Objective**: Understand the subject of animal experiments

| | |
|---|---|
| 1 | Has superficial understanding of the subject. Can refer to a few examples. |
| 2 | Knows about a range of experiments and the purposes for which they are carried out. |
| 3 | Understands the main arguments for and against experiments or has good knowledge of the case either for or against experiments. |
| 4 | Has a thorough knowledge of the subject. Knows some less common arguments related to it. |

## Self-assessment

When arriving at marks to be entered on the Record of Progress, whether it is a formal test or not, there may be times when part or all of the assessment can be carried out by the students themselves. Some categories of skill may lend themselves particularly to this form of assessment (e.g. 'be able to work independently'), though the exercise might on many other occasions prove valuable, since students are generally quite critical of themselves and this can be very productive. Sometimes both teacher and student can assess the performance independently and any discrepancies provide the basis for useful discussion.

Given the trend towards more student autonomy, it is desirable that students should be encouraged to learn and undertake self-assessment progressively as the course develops.

## Internal/mock examinations

With the 'A' level examination as the prime objective for all students, it is important that they are adequately prepared for the examination in every way, including 'exam techniques'. But how far is the practising of examinations essential? To what extent do students have to be fed a diet of 'examination questions' beforehand? The answer to these questions depends to some extent on the format of the examinations, but the boards have recently become more aware of the importance of the link between teaching and examining and in the most progressive syllabuses have made a real effort to structure their examinations in such a way as to promote good teaching practice. Additionally, if the objectives we set are appropriate to the needs of the students, including the need to succeed in a particular examination, then the students will automatically be prepared in an adequate way for that examination. Nonetheless, in the later stages of the course, the working of past papers or papers in the same format as the examination gives students a sense of security as they approach it and it is important that they do feel familiar with the tests they are liable to face. Most teachers set up their mock exams to imitate completely the conditions of the actual examination, and this seems eminently sensible - though where these occur a significant time before the examinations (e.g. the preceding December or January), it might be wise not to expect students to cope with a full examination, since certain skills may still be undeveloped or parts of the content of the syllabus may not have been covered.

Many establishments build into their 'A' level programme an end-of-first-year examination and this should also be carefully thought out. At this stage in the course it is hardly appropriate to set tests equal in difficulty to the 'A' level itself. As with all forms of testing, the objectives must be clearly known in advance by the students and the tasks realistic (i.e. must not catch them unawares). A fair model would give credit for work in all four skills and content. Where no formal requirement for an examination exists, teachers producing Records of Progress as outlined above can draw on these and other results (see below) to give a profile of their students' performance.

Many teachers have used regular testing (e.g. of vocabulary, verbs) as a means of ensuring that specific items are learnt. The results of such tests can be readily absorbed into the Record of Progress, either as a specific section or within another closely related one. If marked, say, out of twenty, the test can easily be translated to the scale of 1-4 and entered in the relevant category of the Record.

**Monitoring of work completion/ marking**

Topic-based courses using the wide range of exercises described in the preceding chapters make very different demands on students compared with traditional courses. Teachers' energies will certainly be channelled in new directions, and as a result the marking of all pieces of work may no longer be appropriate. So much of the work demanded of students will be preparation of texts, the working of reading/listening exercises or preparation for written or oral activities. In this context, different strategies for monitoring students' work have to be adopted.

Provided the course objectives are clearly set and assessment of the kind mentioned above is carried out, teachers and students will have a good idea of the progress which is being made and where particular strengths or weaknesses lie. The assessment can thus become an important part of the learning process. However, on a routine basis teachers will need to be less formal but nonetheless very alert in respect of checking up that work set is indeed carried out. Most teachers will adopt a class approach to going through exercises set as homework. The danger with this is that the students may, inadvertently, consolidate errors by not fully grasping the correct answers. A solution to this is to insist on them always writing their answers in pencil, with the teacher using OHP transparencies to correct the work together in class. This way, students can see the exact wording and spelling of answers, copy them down in ink, and the OHP can go 'into the bank' for future use. Individualised teacher marking can thus be justifiably more selective, concentrating on extended writing, other exercises in which individual responses are likely to vary and non-objective tests. In courses which are student-based, it is important to ensure that the full range of these activities is monitored, and this will include organisation of files, handling of resources, time management and so on.

## KEY POINTS

- Assessment is an essential part of a properly-structured course, making it possible to check whether objectives have been reached
- Assessment should be undertaken at the end of every topic/module of work on the basis of the set objectives
- Assessment should not require students to engage in any task which they are not equipped to carry out
- All the objectives of the course should, at some stage, be subject to assessment
- Assessment should be undertaken on the basis of clearly formulated and understood criteria
- Assessment should be clearly recorded to enable students and staff to gauge progress and take appropriate action
- Assessment could feed into an individual Record of Progress, which might be linked to the Record of Achievement
- Regular testing (vocabulary, grammar) can form part of the assessment pattern and contribute to the Record of Progress
- Assessment should be straightforward to administer and can be linked to routine activities
- Students should be encouraged to undertake self-assessment as and when appropriate
- Internal/mock examinations may play an important part in the assessment and learning process
- As syllabuses are more closely linked to teaching practice, the need for specialised examination technique practice may diminish
- The new syllabuses make new demands on teachers, so that individual marking of all work will not be possible.
- Careful strategies need to be adopted for monitoring of students' progress throughout the course

## Chapter 8

# SUPPORTING A RESOURCE-BASED COURSE

The purpose of this chapter is to look at the organisational and practical issues arising from teaching for the new syllabuses.

**The nature and choice of teaching resources**

Ideally, the courses teachers run for their students are tailored to local, group and even individual needs. Thus, objectives are thought out and set, and material produced to meet those objectives. However, the practical implications of producing an entire in-house course with its supporting materials to cover all the skills and areas outlined in preceding chapters are considerable. In practice, resources are built up - particularly in schools with small sixth forms - very slowly and on a piecemeal basis. The extent to which one can build up an individualised course (i.e. a resource-based course dependent on a whole variety of resources rather than a single course book) will vary greatly, depending on size of establishment, existing resources, budget, staff availability and quantity, access to France, staff experience, etc.

In all likelihood, resources will grow gradually and will almost certainly begin with the use of one of the 'A' level course books currently on the market. The great disadvantage of books is that they are fixed in focus and may very well not cover all the topics prescribed for a particular syllabus. In choosing a course book, it is important to look closely at the subject matter it covers and check on the level of difficulty; some books are designed as first-year courses and therefore should be within the compass of students who have just taken GCSE. It is crucial to ensure that the book covers appropriate topics and that the 'exam topics' are not covered too early in the course, for reasons stated elsewhere. It is also worth looking carefully at the exercise types. Although a book may claim to be forward-looking in its approach and in line with the new syllabuses, it may contain exercises of a fairly traditional nature. Teachers wishing to give their students maximum exposure to the foreign language will need to be wary of books in which English explanations and test-forms play a significant part.

Increasingly, publishers as well as the examination boards themselves are seeing the value of producing dossiers of material relating to individual topics. These are clearly ideal since valuable money can be saved by careful targetting. Teachers should beware, though, of limiting themselves entirely to the use of such packs, unless it is clear that the packs are suitable for use early as well as late in the course. Most 'A' level packs currently available are intended for use in the second year. A good compromise is to look for a special-purpose first-year book, then top this up with work on individual dossiers in the second year. In the early stages of teaching the new-style syllabuses, it is likely that teachers will draw on a range of different sources for their material. Here is an example of a list of topics for a single, sample topic.

**LIST OF RESOURCES**

Topic: L'Ecologie

1 *Actuellement*, Dossier 2, 'L'environnement', pp 18-29

2 *Signes du temps: Vécu,* Chapter 1, 'Protéger la forêt', pp 1-10
*Aperçus*, Chapter 12 'Opération survie', p 187 etc

3 *Nous les Français*, Chapter 4, 'Les Français et l'environnement', pp 32-41

4 *Au courant*, Chapter 2, 'Une seule terre', pp 22-35

5 *Oxford Delegacy Resource Packs*: 'Les parcs nationaux et régionaux'; 'La pollution en France' (E (exam) packs]; 'La sauvegarde de la nature et de l'environnement' [C (coursework pack)]

6 *France Presse*: 'L'homme et sa planète'

7 *Textes et documents pour la classe*: 'La couche d'ozone', 'La pollution atmosphérique', 'La forêt menacée'

8 *Radiovision tape-slide series*: 'Un paysage à protéger: la côte d'Azur'; 'La lutte contre les incendies de forêt'; L'océan menacé'; 'Le parc national de la Vanoise'; 'Que ferons-nous de nos déchets?'

Appendix B contains a selected bibliography of resources for 'A' level French teaching.

**Storing/access/ indexing**

Over a period of time, teachers will probably produce their own exercises based on materials from a great variety of sources to cover the entire course. In larger establishments several teachers may contribute to the ever-growing pool of resources, and it is essential that all the material used in a course should be properly housed, easily traceable and readily available to those who wish to use it.

The first consideration is **storage** and this is linked very closely to the question of **access**. If maximum flexibility is to be achieved, it is most likely that many of the materials will need to be made available for access by students. An initial decision therefore has to be made on what exactly is accessible and by whom. In practice, very few materials need to be restricted to staff use, but where access to them is to be granted to students, it is vital to ensure that a master copy is retained in a secure place for ready access by staff. This is as true for exercises produced on reading texts as it is for video or audio tapes. Valuable articles and other source material can easily be lost if the originals are not kept safe. Any copying (whether photocopying or duplication of a cassette for student use) must of course comply with copyright regulations.

As materials arrive, the next step is to create an **indexing** system which is practical and clear, and which accounts for the different types of resources available. An easy system to operate gives a letter to each type of resource and then an accession number. For example:

| | | |
|---|---|---|
| Reading + text exercises | = | R1 |
| Listening exercises | = | LS6 |
| Speaking activities | = | S24 |
| Writing activities | = | W9 |
| Cassettes | = | C18 |
| Videos | = | V11 |
| Articles (magazine etc with no exercises) | = | A107 |
| OHP transparencies | = | 038 |

(This system could of course be based on the target language, but beware confusion - *Ecrit/Ecoute* etc!)

If such an index system is created from the start, the references can be used to form a valuable database on computer, which students can use when they need to find materials on a given subject for a piece of research or coursework. If it is not possible to compile a database, then a simple 'Index of resources' can be set up under each code letter (R, L etc), or a more sophisticated version could be established with index numbers being entered under various topic headings.

Where items need to be made available for access by students, the easiest way - in the case of texts and exercises - is to store them in clearly labelled wallet folders which keep the different items separate, preferably in a filing cabinet or other receptacle which provides ease of access whilst maintaining a safe and solid place for them to be housed.

In Chapter 6 it was suggested that a topic summary sheet might be produced for each topic. Once a resource bank with student access has been established, the index numbers of each item can be put on the summary sheet. This enables students to collect the relevant items themselves, perhaps as each topic is begun. For this to work efficiently, appropriate numbers of sheets have to be ready well in advance and someone has to take responsibility for this. Where bigger departments exist, members of staff can be responsible for ensuring that different topics are ready for use.

**Learner training**

The great diversity of materials which build up to form a resource bank over even quite a short period makes security a much greater problem than in the past, when it was relatively easy to keep a check on the limited number of books issued. Given the investment in the resources, in terms both of finances and staff effort, it is essential that they are treated with respect and responsibility, though we have to accept that the primary purpose of such resources is to be used.

Initially, it is easy to assume that students will not abuse the system and will treat it in the same way as staff do. It is, however, better to assume that the system will not be properly used unless students are very carefully educated into it. Most of the abuses which can occur, do so through lack of thought rather than deliberate maliciousness. Local rules need to be carefully produced and disseminated, but useful exercises can be produced which take students through the use of the system as it exists in a particular establishment. Nonetheless, the same old faults may recur year after year; items are misplaced in the retrieval system (so that they appear to be lost when they are not), vital copies of a text/tape are removed when other people need to have access to them, all the copies of a text disappear when plenty were made, etc. The importance of respecting the resources is therefore paramount. If individuals or groups of student can be given the responsibility for ensuring the good order of the resources for specific periods, this may help inculcate positive attitudes towards those materials.

## Technological resources

The provision of educational hardware to support our new courses is not always something over which we have control. However, implicit in the new methodology is a desire to make the best use of the resources that are available, and we should remember that student expectations in this area may be quite different now from, say, ten years ago. There is also some hope and expectation that the recommendations of the National Curriculum's Modern Foreign Languages Working Group's advice to the Secretary of State concerning the need to support language teaching with a basic minimum of modern technology will bear fruit. Given the need to ensure that listening skills are developed as effectively as possible, **language laboratories** have come into their own after a period 'out in the cold'. They tend now to be used almost exclusively for receptive listening and enable students to work at their own speed on a pre-recorded tape. Since individual listening is playing an increasing part in 'A' level examinations, this represents a valuable facility. Where laboratories are not available, it is important that students have access at the very least to **personal stereos** which give them a similar facility, though recording sufficient copies of the tape may be a problem. On the other hand, the personal stereo has the added dimension of portability and enables out-of-class listening work to take place.

In the age of television, we cannot escape the importance of **video** as a teaching medium. Schools and colleges lucky enough to have access to a satellite dish are able to use authentic French material on a regular basis - news programmes, documentaries and films. This plays a valuable part in providing insight into French culture and keeping students abreast of contemporary France. One of the big problems for teachers, though, is finding the time to view recorded material to check for usability, and then to prepare for appropriate exploitation. It is well worth reading CILT's publication *Making the most of video* by Brian Hill for a full analysis of the ways in which video can be exploited. The tendency is to assume that its prime purpose is to develop listening, but it also acts as a most effective stimulus to both writing and speaking activities. For schools with access to a video machine (but not a satellite dish), there are many ways of obtaining useful tapes from other sources. A particular danger with video is that it is easy for students to 'turn off' and become at best passive, at worst glazed and non-receptive. Teachers need to be alert to this and to develop strategies which ensure that this is not the outcome of regular exposure to video.

Any teacher who has used Information Technology as part of language teaching will know of the many uses to which it can be put and of its potential as a tool for developing all the skills. This is as true at 'A' level as it is for younger students. The National Curriculum Modern Foreign Languages Working Group's proposals summarise its possibilities as follows:

8.34 IT can stimulate talk in the target language as pupils work together exploring options, asking questions, agreeing responses, testing out ideas and evaluating their actions during any of the activities suggested below. However, some caution needs to be exercised. Computers do not by themselves provide or stimulate talk in the target language, so learners' tasks must be very carefully set up and monitored if any is to take place. Clearly, learners cannot be expected to react to computer programs in the target language if they do not know the appropriate words and phrases, not only for computing but also for the general functions described above. There is no reason, however, why they should not progressively learn them, perhaps aided by the enthusiasm which many feel for IT. In IT as elsewhere, teachers should always beware of tasks which can be completed by native wit rather than by knowledge of the language. In short, the time and expense involved in the use of IT in language lessons needs to be justified, at any rate in the medium term, by a commensurate gain in language competence.

8.35 Nevertheless, properly used, IT can enable learners to:

- use a wider range of authentic material (e.g. satellite TV, on-line databases such as TELETEL or electronic mail and fax);
- access, select, adapt, store, create and present material (e.g. word-processing and text handling, 'concept keyboard', databases, spreadsheets);
- simulate a wide range of situations which involve taking decisions reflecting those in life outside the classroom (e.g. interactive video, computer-based simulations, computer-controlled multi-media activities);
- work at their own pace and at some length on activities and if need be return to them frequently (interactive video, modern language programs, tutorial programs, word-processing, desktop publishing);
- develop their awareness of form and structure. Pupils explore language, reconstructing texts, sequencing words, matching, jumbling, sorting and completing gaps. IT can focus attention on the way the language works, how words relate to each other and how ideas are organised. It can help learners to perceive and use language patterns (e.g. modern language programs which involve manipulating text);
- read and write effectively and present material attractively, especially in the case of learners who have great problems reading, writing and illustrating material. Learners can adapt, write and format text, incorporating pictures and illustrations, confident that the final screen or print-out will be attractive (e.g. interactive multi-media activities, 'concept keyboard', word and sentence building computer programs, word-processing, desktop publishing);
- develop a wide range of strategies, skills and abilities which are useful in the language-learning process but also valuable in themselves. Using IT, pupils can take responsibility for their own learning by planning and collaborating, making and testing hypotheses, summarising, agreeing decisions, etc. In doing so, they develop skills such as using information retrieval and storage systems, decision-making, evaluating, analysis, classification, synthesis, and qualities such as perseverance, self-confidence and independence.

## Finding the time

At the beginning of this chapter, the point was made that the accumulation of resources for a multi-skill, theme-based course is a very gradual process. Teachers starting from scratch should not feel overwhelmed. Although this book advocates a coherent and planned approach, in practice this is very likely to be achieved bit by bit. Many strategies can be adopted for speeding things along; teamwork with colleagues, collaboration within the area or region, exchanging of materials with other schools, using what is already available or can be easily acquired, above all exploiting the enthusiasm and motivation of students - particularly in the collection and organisation of materials. Provided that usable resources are banked and pooled, unnecessary duplication or waste of effort can be avoided. Resources and their management lie at the heart of successful foreign language learning. Time spent on preparing and organising learning materials should not therefore be seen as something additional to the teaching load, but as part of it and an essential part of it. To find this time we may have to devote less time to activities such as marking and to recognise that the shift to more student-centred working will be accompanied by an equivalent alteration to the way we as teachers organise and use our time.

## KEY POINTS

- **A resource-based course takes a long time to build up and is never complete**
- **Any textbook used should be examined closely to see that it relates reasonably to the course's objectives in terms of language and content**
- **Many dossiers are now on the market geared to individual topics, usually for second-year use**
- **Locally-produced resources (exercises etc) need to be clearly indexed, along with other raw materials**
- **Where students have access to materials, security is paramount**
- **Master copies need to be kept of newspaper articles**
- **Computer databases offer the most flexible form of logging**
- **Learner training is vital if resource banks are not to be misused**
- **Technology can be a powerful influence to the good in language learning at this level: video/cassette players/IT**
- **Teamwork and collaboration are essential in building resources**
- **Student-centred learning requires a very different approach**

# APPENDIX A
# LIST OF GRAMMATICAL ELEMENTS/ STRUCTURES

| | |
|---|---|
| □ Verbs: | All regular verbs, including reflexives<br>Common irregulars (less common irregulars - recognition only) |
| □ Verb tenses: | Formation and use of<br><br>indicative<br>(Active): Present, imperfect, future, conditional, past historic (recognition), perfect, pluperfect, future perfect, conditional perfect<br>(Passive): Present, imperfect, future, conditional, perfect, pluperfect<br><br>Subjunctive<br>(Active): Present, perfect<br>(Passive): Present<br><br>Common uses of the subjunctive |
| □ Negatives: | Meaning and position with verbs |
| □ Imperatives: | 2nd singular, 1st plural, 2nd plural |
| □ Present participles: | Formation and use |
| □ Past participles: | Rules of agreement |
| □ Question forms | |
| □ Constructions with infinitives | |
| □ Object pronouns: | Use and position with simple/compound tenses/negatives |
| □ *Quel* etc | |
| □ Adjectives: | Forms, agreements, comparatives, superlatives |
| □ Possessive adjectives: | *mon* etc |

| | | |
|---|---|---|
| ☐ | **Possessive pronouns:** | *le mien* etc |
| ☐ | **Articles:** | Definite, indefinite, partitive |
| ☐ | **Relative pronouns:** | *qui, que, dont, ou, lequel, ce qui* etc |
| ☐ | **Disjunctive pronouns:** | *moi* etc |
| ☐ | **Demonstrative adjectives:** | *ce* etc |
| ☐ | **Demonstrative pronouns:** | *celui* etc |
| ☐ | **Nouns:** | Gender, formation of feminines, plurals |
| ☐ | **Adverbs:** | Types and position |
| ☐ | **Prepositions:** | Differentiation between English and French usage |
| ☐ | **Number:** | Cardinals, ordinals, fractions, prices, measurements, expressions of quantity |

# APPENDIX B
# SELECTED BIBLIOGRAPHY OF RESOURCES FOR 'A' LEVEL FRENCH TEACHING

## A Course Books

- ☐ Corless F and R Gaskell, *Signes du Temps: Vécu* and *Aperçus* (Hodder and Stoughton)
- ☐ Barnes, Donald (ed), *Actuellement* (Stanley Thornes)
- ☐ McEwan, Sue, Gill Pickard, Martin Smith, *Décollage* (GCSE/'A' level bridge) (Stanley Thornes)
- ☐ Brockman, Patrick, Gisèle Guarisco, *Horizons* (Nelson)
- ☐ Rowlinson, William, *Nous les Français* (Parts I and II) (OUP)
- ☐ Moore S, G Pugh and A Antrobus, *Au Courant* (Levels I and II) (Longman)
- ☐ Humberstone, P *Débouchés* (Hodder and Stoughton)
- ☐ Astington E, *Faisons le point* (Heinemann)
- ☐ Limb, Ann and Pam Bourgeois, *Objectifs* (Assignments) (CUP)
- ☐ Beeching, Kate and Isabelle le Guilloux, *Ça se dit et ça s'écrit* (structure and discourse) (OUP)
- ☐ *Cours de français contemporain* (2 levels), various authors (CUP)
- ☐ Beeching, Kate and Brian Page, *Contrastes* (CUP)

## B Periodicals

- ☐ *Actualquarto* (monthly)
- ☐ *Phosphore* (weekly)
- ☐ *Ça m'intéresse* (monthly)

- ☐ *Le Monde dossiers and documents* (selected: monthly)
- ☐ *Le Point* (weekly)
- ☐ *Le Nouvel Observateur* (weekly)
- ☐ *Marie-France* (monthly)
- ☐ *Echos*

## C Reference

- ☐ *Larousse de Poche* (Larousse)
- ☐ *Dictionnaire pratique* (expensive) (Larousse)
- ☐ *La grammaire en clair* by P Roger and J Long (Nelson)
- ☐ *Quid*
- ☐ *Vous avez dit France*, A Kimml

## D Other

- ☐ *Oxford Delegacy Resource Packs* (many titles, including exercises) (UODLE)
- ☐ *Textes et documents pour la classe* (many titles) (CNDP)
- ☐ *Radiovision* (tape-slide series: many titles) (CNDP)
- ☐ *Voix de France* (radio programmes) (BBC)
- ☐ *Actualités radio-presse* (news recordings, texts, exercises) (Macmillan)
- ☐ *Authentik* (news recordings, texts, exercises) (27 Westland Square, Dublin)
- ☐ *Thématique* (Mary Glasgow)
- ☐ Technology in Language Learning series (CILT) (see pp 165-6)

  *Making the most of video*

  *Making the most of IT skills*

  *Making the most of audio*

  *Making the most of your video camera*

  *Making the most of satellites and interactive video*

  *Making the most of micro-computers*